I'll Tell You
in Person

I'll Tell You in Person

. . .

CHLOE
CALDWELL

Coffee House Press
An Emily Books Original
Minneapolis and Brooklyn
2016

Coffee House Press books are available to the trade through our primary dis-
tributor, Consortium Book Sales & Distribution, cbsd.com or (800) 283-3572.
For personal orders, catalogs, or other information, write to info@coffee
housepress.org.

Coffee House Press is a nonprofit literary publishing house. Support from
private foundations, corporate giving programs, government programs, and
generous individuals helps make the publication of our books possible. We
gratefully acknowledge their support in detail in the back of this book.

Library of Congress Cataloging-in-Publication Data
Names: Caldwell, Chloe, author.
Title: I'll tell you in person / Chloe Caldwell.
Description: Minneapolis : Coffee House Press, [2016] | Series: Emily Books
Identifiers: LCCN 2016007063 | ISBN 9781566894531 (softcover)
Subjects: | BISAC: LITERARY COLLECTIONS / Essays. |
   BIOGRAPHY & AUTOBIOGRAPHY / Personal Memoirs. |
   BIOGRAPHY & AUTOBIOGRAPHY / Literary.
Classification: LCC PS3603.A432 A6 2016 | DDC 814/.6—dc23
LC record available at http://lccn.loc.gov/2016007063

Acknowledgments

The author would like to thank the editors of the following publications,
where variations of some essays were first published: *Vice, Salon, Medium,
Hobart,* and the *Rumpus.* In some essays, names and identifying details have
been changed.

Thank you to the Martha's Vineyard Writer's Residency, where pages of this
book were written.

Enormous thank you: Emily Gould for acquiring, encouraging, and constant
support; Ruth Curry for the excellent and attentive edits and honesty. I am
lucky to know you both. Thank you Chelsea Lindman, Caroline Casey, Chris
Fischbach, Carla Valadez, Amelia Foster, Heidi Hogg, and everyone on the
Coffee House team: what an honor to work with such intelligent, kind, and
wonderful people. Thank you to my early readers and responders: Steph
Georgopulos, Fran Badalamenti, Chelsea Martin, Elizabeth Ellen, Karina
Briski, Elisa Albert, Erika Kleinman, and Diana Spechler. Thank you Mom,
and thank you Dad. I love you both.

Printed in the United States of America
23 22 21 20 19 18 17 16   1 2 3 4 5 6 7 8

For my friend Frances Badalamenti

Do you remember the way the girls
would call out "love you!"
conveniently leaving out the "I"
as if they didn't want to commit
to their own declarations.

—DAVID BERMAN,
SELF-PORTRAIT AT 28

◆ ◆ ◆

I get it. Nothin's ever happened to you—
and you write books about it.

—PATRICIA HAMPL'S STUDENT,
THE DARK ART OF DESCRIPTION

Contents

I'll Tell You
in Person

In Real Life

WHAT SHOULD I DO with my life? my notebook from 2005 reads. *Music therapist? Retail/venue owner? Substance-abuse counselor? Writer? But I'm unfocused, unambitious, have an addictive personality, and what if no one cares?*

I've spent the bulk of my years on planet Earth asking for forgiveness rather than permission. I've never had a plan B or F or even A. I don't know how to read maps. Driving with my mom some years ago, I got lost, and rather than stopping or looking at a map, I kept going the wrong way. "When you get lost, you're supposed to pull over and turn around," she said. I do when I'm ready. One editor asked my agent last year what my five-year plan was. I laughed, even though I was the stupid one, not the editor (who rejected the book).

As the cliché goes, I've always counted on either dying young or never dying at all. I displaced my enormous anxiety onto dogs, electrical outlets, Mack trucks running me over, and, apparently, essay collections. I did not imagine my life past thirty, because I thought women in their thirties were magical unicorns, part of a club that didn't want me as a member. But I'm still here—not unhealthy, not unhappy, a little unaffluent. When this book comes out, I will be thirty (and a half, if I can avoid those Mack trucks), and even writing this now, my current life contradicts some of the sentiments in the essays that follow, which I wrote at twenty-five, at twenty-seven, last month. For example, I now have a car and a savings account, and God help me if these additions to my life don't feel incredible— magical-unicorn status, even.

◆ ◆ ◆

I felt my age for the first time last spring. I was sitting at a picnic table at the writing residency I was attending in Martha's Vineyard, and we were talking about having children. One woman, a murder-mystery writer, told us she was eight weeks pregnant. She explained she was getting used to the fact that she couldn't drink or eat oysters. She joked that she couldn't believe and didn't believe she was pregnant. The woman as she knew herself was changing, gone. "I can't do anything fun anymore," she said.

We shared stories of being mistaken for being pregnant. (This has never happened to me. Instead, I get asked if I have children—which I think is worse, since it means I don't look glowing and pregnant: I look like a stressed-out mother with toddlers.)

Anyway, as we discussed this, I offered, "When people ask me if I have kids, I'm like, 'No!' because in my head I'm still twenty-one years old."

What was so disconcerting was the hearty laughter that followed. People *laughed*. My feelings weren't hurt, but I was a little shocked. I wasn't expecting them to say, "Well, you *do* look twenty-one," or "Yeah, me too," but I was surprised when they didn't. It was surprising that they saw me for what I am: An adult. A twenty-nine-year-old. I want to ask something like, is twenty-nine really that different than twenty-one? Of course it is. It makes perfect sense. I am twenty-nine, and I lived the fuck out of my twenties. I even documented it to prove it. That night in the mirror, after taking off my makeup, I put my hair in braids. I was buzzed on wine, my eyes half-moons, and I thought I could see, for the first time, what I would look like as an old, decrepit woman.

◆ ◆ ◆

When I was eighteen and in my final year of high school, I broke into my older brother's bedroom, looking for leftover Halloween candy or quarters to steal. I ended up taking a random book off his bookshelf. There was nothing special about the book that attracted me to it—no reason for me to pull it down. The cover was white and orange, with an etching of a street and a palm tree. It was a 180-page paperback: *Like Water Burning: Issue One*. The book was a small-press anthology, collecting eighteen pieces of writing. Of the eighteen, three of the titles in the table of contents had an asterisk next to them. The asterisk at the bottom of the page read:

Nonfiction tastes best with a bottle of Charles Shaw Cabernet.

Naturally, I turned first to one of the nonfiction pieces because it seemed special and juicy, and I don't believe in reading books in order, a quirk that frustrates most people who know me.

I was painting long before I started writing and longer before I met you, the essay I read first begins. The essay was "Mono No Aware" by a writer named Miki Howald. It is an essay that is simultaneously a love story. The narrator, Miki, is an oil painter who works for the government. She falls in love with a boy who plays baseball and is soon leaving town. The essay is structured around the cherry blossoms outside her window. It is about grief, joy, change, love, and the beauty of transient things.

I can't let go, Miki tells her mother toward the end of the essay, after watching the blooming and dying of the cherry blossoms outside her window over three days.

Hooked. I was hooked. The way her beginning is her ending and her ending is her beginning. The way she zooms in and then out, then back in again. How the last sentence both opens and closes at the same time. The way I could imagine her bare feet on the fire escape and feel her heartache and the way it soothed my own heartache. I wanted to do that. But how did she do that? Take something from her life and craft it into this moving piece of art that resonated with me even though it had nothing to do with me? I inserted myself in the words and made her experience mine. I've learned this notion of not knowing where you end and the artist begins, while watching films and reading books, has a term: *participation mystique*. The concept is closely tied to *projection*.

Returning to the essay now, it is absolutely embarrassing how much I have taken from it. I have used her rhythm and versions of her sentences and sentiments in both of my books and in various essays. I've basically memorized the essay, and sometimes I forget I'm not the one who wrote it.

Once every few years I search for Miki Howald, wanting to tell her how much her essay means to me and wanting to read more of her work. She is less findable than most authors these days are; she has no website or Twitter account. I can't find her e-mail address and have sent her one unanswered Facebook message. When I Google "Mono No Aware by Miki Howald," I find only myself, talking about Miki Howald in an interview. I have attached my name to hers, myself to her. The only facts I know about her personal life are from her biography in the anthology from 2005, which is now out of print. She was living in Alaska, getting her MFA and training for the Iditarod.

"Oh, I absolutely love hearing the details of other people's lives!" Stephanie says in Judy Blume's *Just as Long as We're Together*, a book I read seventeen times through puberty and adolescence.

. . .

"The thing about your essays is that they're always about *you*," a past boyfriend said. "Well, yeah—personal essays are a *genre*," I retorted. "Ever heard of it?"

"I'm trying to be as nice as I can, but I can't stop thinking about your essay where you talk about getting fucked from behind," a different past boyfriend said, after going limp in my mouth. We broke up the next day, and I never saw him again. Bye.

"What are you doing with your life? You should go to school and get a business degree," said another, you guessed it, past boyfriend, after too many Manhattans.

. . .

The liberating thing about publishing an essay collection before you are a fully formed person is that there is nothing to fear. You have no readers. No experience. No memories of doing it before. No wounds. The bad thing about publishing an essay collection at twenty-five, when the frontal lobe has barely finished developing, is there is nothing to fear. No readers. No experience. No memories of doing it before. No wounds.

◆ ◆ ◆

Chicago, Illinois, February 2012, the first place I touched my first collection of essays. I'd taken a painkiller on the morning flight and passed out drooling. I made my way to the *Time Out Chicago* offices and picked up a box of my books. I asked the receptionist to take a photo of me holding my book. I could not juggle my box of books with my rolling suitcase and purse and backpack, so I went to a Chipotle across the street, pounded a burrito, and flipped through the book, staining the pages with guacamole and salsa.

This book was the first project I'd ever finished. At my book release party, I overheard a woman say to my mom, "She's really a go-getter, huh?" and my mom agreed. My heart fluttered when I heard this. The sentence did not align with the way I'd thought about myself and how I presumed others thought about me. I was just coming to terms with my own mediocrity. I'd failed significantly, and I've always been a quitter. I didn't go to school on Career Day in high school, and I have zero degrees. It wouldn't have surprised me if I'd been voted Most Aimless in our senior yearbook.

I sometimes wonder what would have happened had I not published that essay collection, because almost all of my best friends, and everyone I've slept with since then, I met through that book.

◆ ◆ ◆

"It's funny hanging out with you after reading your work. You seem like a monster in your books, but when I hang out with you,

you're, like, the loveliest person," my friend Lauren said to me as we walked through Crown Heights.

"Most of the stuff I wrote about was liquor induced, and I don't drink liquor anymore," I told her. Then, sensing I was hurt, she said, "Maybe *monster* is a little extreme."

The essays in my first collection divulged what most would call TMI. I wrote about how I loved giving blowjobs and that they were a safe place for me (I see what I meant but never had that experience again) and about my frequent masturbation (still often, but less) and how I liked to eat burgers with blue cheese after orgies (never again had an orgy and probably never will but I stand by burgers after sex—no bun, though, as I'm on my gluten-free high horse, and salad instead of fries, please). I wrote about using headphones during sex (sounds fun now). I said I disliked my legs and loved my stomach because weight didn't go to my stomach (it does now, sucker!).

Maybe six months after *Legs Get Led Astray* came out, my mother and I were driving home from shopping. She twisted her hair around her finger as she always does while driving and said, "I'm at peace with the book now." As for my dad, I put hot-pink Post-its all over his copy and wrote *Skip* on them. For my nana's copy, I straight up ripped out the essay about an orgy and the essay about masturbating. This copy was the PG version and the version passed around to my younger cousins.

My nana then sent me a handwritten letter, which was long and moving, and said she'd thought her twenties were hard, living through World War II, but now she sees the twenties are hard regardless of your situation.

◆   ◆   ◆

Then you experience the second half of your twenties. Your hair grows longer or you chop it short. You learn how to cook rice properly (pretty much). You let your belly-button ring fall out and the hole closes up. You fall in love with a woman. You make kale chips. One friend has a heart attack and another has a baby.

You move into an apartment with a bathtub and trees outside your bedroom window. You find cocaine disgusting, and nothing will go up your nose again. Cigarette smoke makes you want to die. You talk about what you learned in therapy, and you go to bed before eleven p.m. each night. You learn to say no sometimes, instead of defaulting to yes.

I can't let go.

You hold on really tight until you're forced to learn to let go of the ideas you had about yourself. You learn you are a mercurial human being and *never* and *always* and declarations change.

But you're still you. You still get a tattoo on your wrist in Miami because you can. You still binge eat when your roommate is out of town. You still have sex with the wrong people once in a while after taking shots of tequila. You still get cystic acne. You still are a monster at times, just not as frequently. It's less of a lifestyle and more of a personality flaw. You pay your electric bill. You schedule pap smears and dentist appointments and actually go.

. . .

After five years of serious waffling, I decided, with a heavy heart, not to go to school for business. Just kidding! As if. I didn't consider it, obviously. Can you imagine?

Write about what you can't shut up about, David Shields says.

We are called "selfish," "self-indulgent," "masturbatory," and "navel-gazers." Our family and friends are pitied, and it's recommended we stop writing and immediately seek therapy, Jay Ponteri says.

The reason it's very easy for me to write about myself is that I know I'm just like everybody else, Elizabeth Wurtzel says.

When I was writing my first essay collection, I felt no shame. But now, because of the repercussions, or people being able to Google me and read about my acne, my sex life, my family, I feel shame. Who do I think I am to write about myself? Who do I think I am to be so solipsistic? Who the fuck am I?

One morning at the residency, I took a walk with my friend Karina. The weather was the kind I hate, overcast and ominous. I broke down crying. "It's too hard," I said. I felt like I was using too much of myself in my work. What could I save for just me?

"I don't have . . . *stories*," Karina said later on our walk (we'd gotten lost, not knowing how to navigate Martha's Vineyard) when we were talking about pitching magazines. I agreed. I do not have "crazy stories" or compelling anecdotes that have happened to me that sound good or interesting or pitch-worthy on paper. I've never gone skydiving or had cancer or rode fast through the countryside of France on the back of a motorcycle belonging to a man I just met at a bar. I've never been divorced or donated my eggs or cut my wrists or had a baby. This is why the personal essay form is my favorite. I don't have to have crazy, pitch-worthy *stories* to do it. I don't have to have done shit—I only have to exist and have feelings and observations.

In the television series *Six Feet Under*, my favorite antiheroine, Brenda Chenowith, sits on her bed with her computer. She hallucinates these sentences on the screen:

Go ahead, write.
What exactly do you have to say that hasn't been said before?
All you do is observe yourself.

◆ ◆ ◆

Growing up, my mom kept stacks of memoirs near her bedside. But my dad has an adverse reaction to most memoirs and mumblecore movies starring a strong female lead who makes "poor decisions," as he calls them.

"Chloe loves tragedy," he likes to tell people. "She loves train wrecks."

"Why would you want to read or watch someone continually make stupid choices?" he'll ask at the dinner table.

"Why *wouldn't* you?" my brother will retort.

"Because it's exactly like my life!" I'll say.

"True," my dad laughs. He used to say I led a charmed life, that every time I fucked up, I was taken care of, like when I showed up for one of my flights across the country two hours late—I had the time wrong in my head—they put me on another flight without a problem.

"All essay collections could be called the same thing," he said once. *Feel Sorry for Me: I Fucked Up Eighteen Times and I'm About to Do It Again.*

Sure, I am writing here about myself. Duh. But that's not the point of this book or these essays. I hope you will project your mistakes and failures and heartaches and joys onto mine. I hope you will feel a touch of participation mystique while reading about my sometimes poor decisions. Unless you're perfect. In which case . . .

◆ ◆ ◆

I'm the type of person who doesn't change the clock back in her car, the type who instead waits for spring to come around again. I'm also the type of person who gets mistaken for an employee no matter where I am: the Gap, a coffee shop, a bookstore, an Applebee's. People come up to me and expect me to wait on them. "I don't work here," I say. But I used to. I quit or got fired from everything. Failing and quitting and not showing up were my resting states. I missed so many gym classes that the teacher made me walk the track fifty times before I could graduate. When I worked at a clothing shop on the Upper West Side, I saw an e-mail from the cooperate manager to the store manager, reviewing the staff's lateness. After listing how many times each employee had been late, the manager continued, "But Chloe takes the cake, being ten to twenty minutes late for every single one of the forty-five shifts she's worked."

I quit community college and piano and soccer and the grave-yard shift at Old Navy. At some jobs, I was so horrendous at adding up the day's total or the bill, I lied and said I was dyslexic. "Oh, that explains it," my bosses would say. The one time I really shined in anything school related was during the spelling bee in second grade when everyone was impressed with my ability to spell the word *agriculture*.

My point is: when I read "Mono No Aware," I realized I'd found something I didn't want to quit, something I desired, something I wanted to show up for: an asterisk next to my name that read: *Nonfiction tastes better with a bottle of Charles Shaw Cabernet.*

So fuck you, Miki Howald, whoever and wherever you are. You cursed me with the personal essay epidemic. Also: Thank you. You introduced me to what I feel most comfortable doing, even though at times it is painfully uncomfortable.

PART I

Prime Meats

AT TWENTY YEARS OLD, unemployed, irreverent, and without a college diploma, I spent my days going on an array of interviews around New York City. I'd had two jobs already—one at a café in Williamsburg and one at a costume jewelry store near Columbus Circle. Both places shut down by leaving notes on their doors, so I was back at zero.

I wore the same outfit (*outfit* is being generous) to my interviews: my friend Ana's polka-dot cotton dress from H&M stained with blue paint and a lace shawl I'd bought on clearance at Buffalo Exchange. Every job I applied for, I found on Craigslist. I took a shot of vodka before my interview at Brooklyn Industries on Bedford Avenue, where the tragically hip manager who interviewed me asked, "What was the last show you went to?" and I choked, too buzzed to think clearly. I took the train to Grand Army Plaza to interview to work for a children's gymnastics class. Nope and nope. I interviewed at Zara (borrowing my dominatrix roommate's fancy pink dress for that one, feeling like a *real woman* as I walked down Broadway) and at Beacon's Closet where a cross-eyed girl grilled me on the latest fashion trends. I didn't know. Stripes? I interviewed at a temp agency and as a cocktail waitress at a gentleman's club (I was so naive, I wore my polka-dot dress for that interview too). I considered nude modeling for a charcoal-drawing class at a loft in Bushwick—went as far as to meet the instructor and look at the space, but every time he e-mailed me to schedule my slot, I'd pussy out.

Then: I scored on Craigslist. I was hired full time as a salesgirl for an independent jewelry designer. The jewelry designer owned two shops across from each other on Bleecker Street ("Between

Grove and Barrow Streets," I said eight times a day in a sweet and patient voice when people called, lost).

I was lucky to find a full-time job in New York City that paid twelve bucks an hour and gave me forty hours a week. "We hired you because when you came for your interview, you talked a *lot*," the other salesgirls later told me. (Those vodka shots I took before interviews were finally working in my favor!)

I worked at the flagship store selling sterling silver and gemstones. In the back of the shop was the jewelry designer's studio where she carved her new designs out of wax and blasted Tupac and drank bubble tea. She wore black zip-up hoodies with her full name on them in white gothic font and white wifebeaters with her name on them in black gothic font. She gave me one of each when I was hired, and I lived in them.

The designer—who I'll call Lisa—was the daughter of Chinese immigrants, born and raised on the East Coast. She'd worked successfully on Wall Street for many years but quit and changed her career path. She was petite, maybe five-foot-two, and buff. The kind of person who pretends she doesn't work out, but does every single day, as Ana put it. I described her to people as a "swift orange-eater," which always got a laugh. She did peel and eat oranges *really* fast.

Lisa lived with her husband in an apartment a few doors down from the shop. Her husband liked to say I had a "gift for gab." He was a construction worker by day and performed in a metal band by night. Our staff often went to his shows at Arlene's Grocery and Trash Bar.

Lisa was intense going on scary. She assigned us books to read (*How to Win Friends and Influence People* and *The Gift of Fear*), and we had unpaid staff meetings to discuss them. She sent e-mails about the women who lived above the store who complained about our loud music with the subject line *Lesbian Upstairs Bitches*. It was Lisa's e-mails and texts that I fell asleep and woke up to each day for three years:

If a baker is evaluated by how many loaves he bakes (that are sellable), what would you consider a numerical measure(s) of what you do?

I ONLY HAD MEN *looking at our Dior and Louis Vuitton bags yesterday. And, they were* NOT GAY MEN *either! They were* ALL GHETTO. *I don't like this male attention we are getting, so* PLEASE *be careful and do* NOT *let peeps in the shop if they do not look right.*

Chloe, you need to get rest and stop worrying about your life. It will work out naturally. Your path will reveal itself each day and you won't even realize you're on it till later.

You did not want to get on her bad side, so I didn't. I was—somehow—a natural at selling jewelry and hit the sales goals each month. It's safe to say I was her favorite. At our weekly staff meetings she'd say, "How come Chloe can sell so much jewelry and the rest of you can't?" and my face would turn bright red. She had nicknames for all of her employees and she called me Chlo-Po. At the end of every single shift we had to send her an e-mail describing what we did and didn't do that day.

For my twenty-first birthday Lisa gave me a card thanking me for being so earnest as well as fifty dollars, which I blew immediately on a martini at the Art Bar and the sketchy palm-reading place across the street from it.

Lisa and I flew to Los Angeles together to sell jewelry at a sales event called "Girl Party" at either Jennifer Garner's or Anne Hathaway's house—I get them confused. We ate edamame on the floor and watched MTV at night. Before bed, I wrote in my journal, and Lisa read *The Razor's Edge* by W. Somerset Maugham.

"I can literally *feel* myself getting smarter and my brain expanding while I read this!" she exclaimed.

Lisa was the only woman in my life who was in her thirties, unless you count the bartender at Wogies. Wogies was a sports bar my friend Ana and I went to out of convenience. Wogies was the opposite of the bars we usually went to. Like everything we did, going to Wogies began as a joke, and then a year went by and it turned into our life. When we went to Wogies, we never ordered the Philly cheesesteak they were known for; instead we ordered carrot sticks and celery with a side of blue cheese, but no wings. We wanted to stay slim. We charged this dinner to Ana's credit card most of the time.

The shop was not my second home, but my first home. I kept a toothbrush and deodorant in the bathroom cabinet and a box of oatmeal on a shelf in the back room. I shaved my legs in the sink before going out. I worked forty hours a week, from noon to eight, which was perfect for my lifestyle. I could go out as late as I wanted, and no matter how psychotic my night was, I could make myself presentable for work. Throw on a dress, take a few Advil, grab a bagel or bialy and coffee on the street corner. The writer Naomi Wolf lived in the neighborhood and often came in the store to drop off her tangled jewelry, which I would untangle with pins and a headlamp on a velvet tray. I had not heard of Naomi Wolf, but after someone told me she was a writer, I became flustered whenever she came in. We didn't charge her anything to untangle her jewelry, though it took hours, eventually pissing us all off, and Lisa instated a policy that we wouldn't untangle jewelry for free anymore.

◆ ◆ ◆

What I learned selling jewelry: even in jewelry shops, women are weird about their bodies. They complain or apologize for their imperfect earlobes while trying on earrings, and I heard the statement "I have tiny wrists" a dozen times a day, even when these women's wrists were totally average in size. It's like our wrists are the only body parts we can genuinely say are tiny, and it makes us feel good. I also heard "Rings are for ourselves, necklaces are for everyone else." "Gold is for the winter, silver is for the summer." There were women who were depressed about their birthdays and came in to buy themselves a piece of jewelry. Their cell phones rang with people wanting to wish them happy birthday, and they ignored the calls. I learned some great tips about jewelry: nothing is sterling silver unless it's stamped with "925" or a logo, you can clean your jewelry with aluminum foil and boiling water and baking soda, and mixing metals is actually cooler than matching.

. . .

Two years after Lisa hired me, she deemed me responsible enough to manage another employee. She hired my best friend to be my right-hand woman. When Ana was hired, Lisa bumped me to the higher-end store across the street and gave me a raise, and Ana took my place at the silver shop. We were often alone in our respective stores, and since Lisa was hypervigilant, she left one pit bull in each store for protection. Their names were Prada and Viper. We were scared shitless of them. They barked loudly when customers came into the store, especially men.

Lisa e-mailed: *We have to keep the dogs away from peeps,* EVEN *if the customers say they are fine with dogs. The downside to the dogs being in the store is that* ANYONE *can sue us for anything related to the dogs. And right now, PitBulls will be put down with any human disturbance. Yes, even some peeps do not like puppies.*

I was one of those peeps, but I kept that to myself.

Lisa was always stressing dramatically about something. When all the girls at the shop signed up to receive their DailyOM horoscope each day (I still get it), she said it would make her too stressed out to see it in her inbox. She was constantly telling us how much she spent on office supplies—once even threatening to fire one of us if we didn't cut back on our use of printer paper. She invested in high-end walkie-talkies for the employees to use in emergencies. Ana and I talked on them for six of the eight hours that constituted a shift. We'd stand across the street from each other smoking shittily rolled cigarettes, singing, talking, joking on our walkie-talkies.

One morning when we showed up for work, Lisa took Ana and me aside.

"I saw you guys walking down the street with Discmans last night, so I wanted to give these to you. The kids don't use them."

The *kids* she was referring to were her stepchildren, and what she was giving us were two slightly used iPod shuffles.

• • •

Ana and I were highly imaginative when we drank, and for Lisa's birthday, we had this idea that we should sneak into the store and paint the wooden floor the company colors: purple and yellow. I had a key to the shop, a privilege I abused. One night after drinking at Wogies, we bought purple and yellow paint at Pearl, then snuck into the store and painted what looked like a magic carpet, Aladdin style, on the floor as a surprise. While we painted we listened to the only album I liked to listen to when I drank: Jimmy Fallon's "Troll Doll Jingles Medley" on an album called *The Bathroom Wall* that we borrowed from Ana's mom. In the morning we were worried we'd get fired for painting on the floor, but Lisa seemed to appreciate it.

Ana and I had another way we amused each other: surveys. We wrote surveys with funny titles and e-mailed them to each other. The questions were totally random, from *What street from your life did you wake up the happiest on?* to *How many times have you had anal sex, and how many times do you think Obama has had anal sex? Would you rather sit next to Woody Allen or Obama on an airplane and why?* Since we had free access to printers, we started printing out the questions in bulk—ignoring Lisa's aggro e-mails to cut back on paper usage. After work, we brought them to bars and handed them out to strangers. They were a hit. We often had groups of people around us asking, "Can I have one?" "What are these for?" "What do you do with the information?" "Do you work for *The L Magazine?*"

What with the surveys, the hangovers, and the walkie-talkies, Ana and I slowly became more and more horrendous at our jobs. One night we wanted to go out for drinks but didn't have enough money because we were waiting for our paychecks to clear. We had a plan: go to the bar anyway and drink until midnight. At midnight our paychecks would hit our accounts and we would pay with our debit cards. We drank from eight until midnight. Both of our cards were declined. We went back to the jewelry store, unlocked it, and pushed the heavy gate up together. The alarm went off. The alarm company called and asked me the password. "Diamonds," I said. We unlocked the petty-cash box and took enough out of it to cover our fifty-dollar tab. I snuck in early a few days later to replace the money. Another time we snuck back into the store, too drunk to make it home, and slept on the floor of the shop together underneath a fur coat we'd found. If Lisa had walked by with her dogs in the morning, we probably would have been fired. I say *probably* because as unprofessional as Ana and I were, Lisa needed us, and we came through for her—we worked on Christmas Eve and Christmas Day. I didn't call in sick once for the three years I worked there.

That spring we were on a terrific and terrifying bender. I was leaving New York at the end of April and knowing this motivated us take our already ludicrous antics up a notch. We'd go seven days in a row sleeping at either Ana's apartment on Troutman Street in Bushwick or mine on Seaman Avenue in Inwood. Ana bought silk black sheets I always slid off of while we slept. She could only fall asleep to Hole's *Celebrity Skin* album or the songs "Got You (Where I Want You)" by the Flys and "Swallowed" by Bush. We never argued with each other; we were only endearing and enabling. All you need is one person in the world to condone your horrifying behavior, and to each other, we were that one special person. When we wanted to get home before four a.m. we wore heels. That way our feet would hurt, and we'd go home at a respectable time. This plan never worked, but we thought it was genius.

On my twenty-third birthday, I walked to a lingerie store near my apartment in Inwood and bought a see-through red bra and some mint gel to use for blowjobs as an impulse purchase. I took the A train to meet Ana at Wogies. We sat at the bar and downed some Bloody Marys and she gave me my gift—an identical T-shirt to the one she was wearing—white with "New York City" written on the front. I began writing a list called *Reasons*

Why I Suck and thought I was really liberated and radical for doing this. But Ana quickly became annoyed. "Are you going to do this all day?" she asked.

That night, Ana and I went to a house party and stole a fifth of Bacardi out of the kitchen. We carried it with us for the following week. That Sunday at the jewelry store, Lisa left early. We decided to start drinking some rum out of coffee cups. This was risky because there were cameras in both stores, and Lisa sometimes watched the footage.

I started looking at Craigslist and reading the ads out loud over the walkie-talkie to Ana. A few days before Saint Patrick's Day we posted an ad inviting strangers to meet us at Wogies to drink and party with us. When the night came, though, we sat at a booth getting hammered with Lisa and her husband, not knowing if any of the guys we invited showed up and not giving a shit either way.

◆　◆　◆

Ana and I loved the concept of steak and scotch. Steak and scotch equaled ultimate decadence, which our lives lacked. In reality we ate Sabra hummus and carrots, chased down with Wild Turkey whiskey. We never bought bread when we got groceries because we didn't want to get fat. We did not have partners to take us out to dinner. We lived on black coffee and quinoa with nothing in it. And the people we knew who were able to afford steak and scotch were men who lived in Manhattan. But we didn't know these men. So we went where you go for anything you need: Craigslist. We posted a photo of us together, shit-faced and wearing head-dresses, and this ad:

Steak and Scotch
Hey sexy bros, who wants to buy some prime bitches some prime meat and drink obscene amounts of liquor? Let's kick it.
P.S. *We're psycho (in a fun way) and we want to give you surveys.*

We received a bunch of responses. After e-mailing back and forth with some guys, we decided that the man who seemed the most accommodating and safe was Alex Berman. He claimed he had weed and liquor and said that if we were "for real" we could come over. He lived in Chelsea on Twenty-Third Street. We made plans with two other guys we would meet after Alex, and some other guys later in the week. We wrote a survey we called "Steak Frenzy Survey" and printed out a few copies.

We were giddy as we walked arm in arm to Chelsea. We were dressed the same—Levi "boyfriend jeans," American Apparel v-necks, and backpacks. Ana wore a hat made of brown rabbit fur with ears coming down all the way to her chest, and I wore a black-and-white trucker hat. It was April, blossoms on the trees, and finally, it was bright out at six o'clock. We knew we were getting some scotch out of the deal, but Alex hadn't mentioned anything about steak.

"Dude, if you feel weird, just look at me or something, and we'll leave," I told Ana. That was our grand plan for if Alex Berman was a psycho killer or rapist: *just look at me.*

Alex lived in a condominium. When he answered the door, he looked us up and down.

"How old are you guys?"

"I know we look really young," I said. "But we're twenty-three and twenty."

The sentence hung while he sized us up.

Alex was forty-three and nondescript, with brown hair and brown eyes. I could never pick him out of a crowd today. His apartment was a bachelor's place, with leather couches and music equipment everywhere. He said he was a jazz musician. We sat on Alex's leather couch, and he packed a bong. Ana and I were totally aggressive and hyper even after smoking pot. We asked him our survey questions, and I jotted down his answers. Alex went to the kitchen to grab some orange juice and a bottle of Jack Daniels. His cell phone rang. We heard him say, "Dude, this is funny. I'm looking for a date on Craigslist, and I suddenly have the Census Bureau after me." We drank his pint of Jack with him, shot after shot, swigging orange juice as a chaser.

I went to the bathroom and was shocked when I saw the bathtub—it was so filthy it was completely black. Even he knew it was strange, and when I returned to the living room he apologized for it. I was embarrassed and sad for him. He obviously hadn't had any women over in a long time. But Ana and I were breaking that spell.

Alex said he was going to invite some friends over "to jam" and that we should stay and hang out. Ana and I looked at each other. We told Alex we had to venture on, but maybe we'd come back later. Once alone in the elevator Ana said, "I was thinking how funny it would have been if I'd gone to the bathroom and came out naked." I laughed and agreed. I'd been thinking about what it would have been like to have sex with Alex Berman too.

Next we walked to the East Village to meet a guy whose name I don't remember and possibly never knew. As we climbed the stairs to his apartment I had a familiar feeling. I looked at Ana. "Wait, I feel like we've been here before," she said. We *had* been there before. We'd actually been at that same exact apartment with that same exact guy months ago for a party, invited by a mutual friend. We hung out with him, smoked more weed, gave him the steak survey, and when he went to the fire escape to smoke a cigarette, we chugged some of the gin he had in his kitchen and left.

Finally, we met the guy that would actually buy us steaks. We met him in the West Village, and I was a hungry mess by this time. All I remember about the guy who bought us steaks and French fries and Johnnie Walker Red was that he was from California and had moved to New York the year before but was having a hard time meeting people. Ana took over socially and saved the day. I don't remember getting home that night, but in the morning I woke up with the Californian's survey answers in my purse:

What is the most ultimate steak experience you've ever had?
    Wow, I really like Outback. I've actually gone here in Manhattan a couple of times even though there are so many awesome local

nonchain restaurants. I had an awesome steak at Blue Ribbon Bistro where my buddy works. Worth the more-than-thirty-five-dollars I paid. I had an amazing steak once that was soaked in JD and grilled over an open flame while I was a young Marine. God bless the troops!

How would you feel about incorporating steak into your sex life?

Never have, but thanks for the idea. Kind of makes me think about Hannibal Lector from *Silence of the Lambs* though. Not very sexy.

Have you ever watched porn while eating steak?

Not yet. This survey is full of useful ideas.

A couple of days later, we were still on our rum-and-Craigslist kick. I was Gchatting with my mom at the store with Ana reading over my shoulder, and I made the mistake of telling her what I was up to.

I'm addicted to CL, I said.

What's CL?

Craigslist.

OMG, she responded. *Who/what/where?*

Ana and I go to men's apartments to see what they look like and we bring surveys.

My mother seemed intrigued for a few minutes, saying OMG and *You freak!* but I could almost feel when she changed her mind and realized this was maybe dangerous. Ana and I stared at the little Gchat window where it said *Michele is typing . . .* Finally we heard the familiar ding.

Not safe, she wrote.

At all.

Ana and I leaned into each other, laughing and clutching our sides. It was so simple yet profoundly true. I knew this, but I argued with my mother anyway. I told her people do it every day alone, and Ana and I were doing it together! I told her it was fascinating! I told her if we get a weird vibe we run away!

She responded: *You don't know enough stories of women murdered in* NYC. *You always think you are safe, but you are not in a public place, and you have no idea who this person is or who he told to come over before you get there. I know you think this is just "mom talk," but it's not. What you are doing is risky behavior, and someday you won't be able to run away. Knives and guns have a lot of power, and you will do what the person wants. I know I cannot stop you, you will do what you want, but you should try to get your kicks in a safer way, is my opinion.*

I know, I told her.

And if you are going to these men's apartments, they think you are loose and not smart, so they have ideas of taking advantage of you.

Yeah, maybe, I responded. *But it's under the strictly platonic section. I tell the guys before I get there I am just coming to conduct a survey. It has nothing to do with sex.*

Well, good luck, but those are words. Do a survey, it's great fun and art or whatever. But I bet most artists don't visit unknown strangers in a strange an unknown environment.

I don't know if it was my mother's concern or if I coincidentally lost interest, but I did stop shortly after that conversation.

◆　◆　◆

During my last few days working at the jewelry store, I was apartment-sitting at my sort-of boyfriend Simon's place in the East Village on Ninth Street. Ana and I sat eating breakfast on the stairs outside; it felt like summer now. We watched a man try to go into the printing shop across the street, but it was locked. He turned around and saw us.

"Hey—it's *you* guys!"

Ana greeted him enthusiastically. "Oh my God, hey!" I was dumbfounded for more than a few minutes while they spoke amiably. Finally I whispered to Ana, "Who is he?"

"I'm the *steak and scotch guy!*" he said. "Come on . . . I bought you a steak and French fries—you don't even remember me?"

He had a point. He could have been anyone. Someone I slept with or someone I worked for. In my brain later that day I couldn't stop thinking of him—he morphed into all different kinds of men: a rapist, a sadist, a religious nut, an asshole, or a nice guy. I actually had no idea what kind of man this guy was. Yet I'd eaten a steak dinner with him. He'd seen me cry. *Not safe. At all.* The words rang in my ear. We all laughed and went across the street for coffee. I had my guard up the entire time.

Yodels

MY FATHER USED TO DRIVE a beat-up blue Toyota van. The brakes had to be pumped to actually brake, and there were patches of rust on the body. Later, I'd be embarrassed by this, but as a kid I loved riding next to my dad and listening to Dusty Springfield on the tape deck. The Tic Tacs sat under the tape deck. I loved (and I don't use the word *loved* here lightly) the orange flavor but would settle for spearmint. I never wanted one Tic Tac—I wanted two, then four, then eight. I was six years old. One of my first memories is overhearing my dad, amused, tell my mom he would buckle me in, give me a Tic Tac, then walk around to the driver's side. In those seven seconds I was alone, he explained, I'd already crunched and swallowed the Tic Tac and was reaching for more.

More.

My older brother was the one who could eat with moderation. We were polar opposites from the day I was born. Me: blond and gregarious, and him with his dark eyes and hair and painfully shy personality. I answered for him. I ate for him. On Easter and Christmas, my brother would save much of the chocolate we were given by the Easter Bunny and Santa. I'd stuff all of mine in my face the same day. I'd be jealous for the rest of the year when he'd come home from school and eat some of his chocolate bunny, and I'd have nothing. On Christmas Eve, I'd set my alarm for four a.m. When it went off, I'd creep into the living room and quietly pull my stocking down from the mantel. I'd take everything out of it and bring some chocolate back to my bedroom after putting the rest back into the stocking so I could act surprised in the morning. But my mom always knew, anyway. Halloween? Forget about it.

In no particular order, here are some foods I've binged on: Yodels. Tic Tacs. String cheese. Black licorice. Brie. Refried beans. Cheddar cheese. Freihofer's chocolate chip cookies. Champagne. Ice cream. Coffee. Soda. Quisps. Frosted Flakes. Apple Cinnamon Cheerios. Orange juice. Hot chocolate powder. Kraft macaroni and cheese. Annie's macaroni and cheese. Marshmallows. Mozzarella. Chocolate chips. Wint O Green Life Savers. Peeps. Hot Tamales. The Hot Tamales—I ate them so often, so fast, that for my twenty-third birthday, my dad sent me a package containing fifty king-size packages of them. It was more of a joke present, but I ate them—sometimes a whole box for dinner.

Yodels were the most salacious treats we were allowed in my house when I was growing up. I remember the junk food drawer—it was the bottom drawer, to the left of the fridge. I'd open it with my toes by grasping around the white knob and pulling to check what was in there. Now it's full of Tupperware. Part of the fun is there are so many ways to eat Yodels: You can bite into them and eat them like a hot dog. You can peel off the outer coating of chocolate and eat that separately. Or my favorite way: you can stick your tongue into the hole of the Yodel and get the white stuff out. This is not supposed to sound sexual; it's not my fault it does.

Here was the problem—my mom let us have one Yodel. But Yodels came packaged in two. Like, in my brown-paper-bag school lunch, I'd pull out my sandwich, my apple, and my one Yodel my mother had taken out of the package and put in a little baggie of its own. My brother had the other one. Oh, how this made me want to eat two of them. When I was twelve, my mom, my brother, and I stayed in a house in Cape Cod with my mom's friend and her daughters. We had Yodels in the house. The Yodels taunted and tempted me, and when I was alone in the house briefly, I pounded four of the packages as quickly as I could. This turned into a mystery. "Who ate all of the Yodels?" my mother kept demanding. I never told. Eating them was a way to do something I knew I wasn't supposed to do. It was a secret that could be only mine, and it was a way I could have more than everyone else. More than was acceptable.

My taste buds were a little bit off, like I was born with a broken palate. I liked bananas while they were still green, spaghetti before it was cooked, and hot chocolate not all the way mixed so I could eat the wet powder.

There was always music playing in the living room when I was a kid. One of the musicians we listened to a lot was Loudon Wainwright, especially that song, "The Swimming Song." *This summer, I swam in the ocean and I swam in a swimming pool. Salt my wounds, chlorine my eyes, I'm a self-destructive fool. A self-destructive fool.* When my mom was in a good mood she danced to this and sang along. I have a clear visual memory of her pointing at me singing, *Self-destructive fool.*

There are so many components to eating: it's stress relief, a way to avoid feelings, a way to be mean to yourself, until you realize food is meant to nourish you. I liked to push myself. How far can I go? How many slices of pizza can I eat and not die? How many Yodels until I hate myself?

I haven't been binge eating my entire life; it ebbs and flows. When I was eight years old, I had a friend named Sasha. Our favorite game was "Doctor." We'd have some kind of candy—Sour Patch Kids or Skittles or whatever—and we'd sit on the floor saying, "The doctor told us to only have one! Oh well!" Then we'd laugh maniacally and pour the box into our mouths. I still do this. I did it last night with those adult gummy vitamins. They advise you to take two. I ate ten. (They taste good! I couldn't help it!)

It's not that my parents didn't allow sugar. We weren't vegetarians or vegans or anything hardcore. But candy and soda were not abundant at my house. Neither was sugary cereal. The most sugary cereal we were allowed, on special occasions only, was Apple Cinnamon Cheerios, and the box would be gone in two days. (My brother joined me in that binge.) At other friends' houses, seeing boxes of Lucky Charms and cans of Sprite made my heart leap and made me motivated to sleep at their houses.

My mother is a mindful eater. She eats like a bird. Proportional. "The darker it is, the healthier it is for you," she'd say. At the dinner table, whenever we had a baguette (French bread, we called it), my mother and I had a routine. She'd eat the crust of the slice and hand me the soft white dough. I'd roll it into a ball. I always liked the gross parts of food, the kind with more calories, the kind my mother wouldn't buy. My mother stayed away from anything artificial. I loved *orange* things: candy corn, orange Crush soda, Butterfingers, Kraft cheese, and Cheez Doodles. Finally, when my parents separated, my dad kept Cheez-Its at his apartment. I ate them standing up, by the handful.

I ate—I eat—fast. Torture for me was that game "How many licks does it take to get to the center of a Tootsie Pop?" I don't want to fucking know. Even now, just thinking about it makes my skin crawl. I put lollipops in my mouth and bit down immediately. I chewed, never sucked. This came up even in adulthood, eating with friends, putting dinner mints in our mouths, only for them to hear me loudly crunch down on mine. "Did you already eat yours?" is something I got used to hearing. "Yes, I already ate mine," was something I had to become comfortable with saying.

In high school, I often hung out at my friend Amber's house. Her mother left bowls of candy around as decorations. Amber and her mother didn't even eat from them. This baffled me. How does one leave a bowl of candy out and not eat the entire bowl in one sitting? They always generously offered some to me, and after holidays, Amber would bring me the candy she got, because she didn't want it.

As I got older, I noticed the other thing I didn't grow up around: orange prescription bottles. In 2003, when I was seventeen, I camped for a weekend with Amber at Berkfest, which is a huge druggie music festival in Massachusetts. The trail known for having the most and best drugs was called "Shakedown." We walked down it—we stuck out like sore thumbs; we were dressed up and we didn't have dreadlocks—and we took everything we were handed. Acid, ecstasy, nitrous, mushrooms. Amber and I recently had a conversation about this. "Would we have done bath salts?" we both wondered aloud, flabbergasted at our own naiveté and recklessness. That was the final year Berkfest was held. There were too many overdoses.

When Amber dropped me off at home after the festival, I went to my bedroom and wailed. I was tired and creaky and hungover and depressed. I'd had realizations on the acid: drugs were for imbeciles. I'd never do a drug again, I wrote in my journal.

I did, of course. Of course I did. I did drugs again and again, looked for them and found them. I thought drug habits were something only people who had their shit together could sustain, and I was one of those people. Tic Tacs turned into Klonopin, Adderall, hydros. I took two, three, five.

I slipped through life with no major consequences, mental or physical, from my casual drug use. Unlike other people, I thought, I was able to dabble. Now I realize that the word wasn't *dabble*, it was *replace*. I replaced weed with mushrooms. Mushrooms with acid. Acid with ecstasy. Ecstasy with Adderall. Adderall with cocaine. Cocaine with speed. Speed with OxyContin. And when drugs weren't available there was always alcohol. Food. Sex. I was a grabber. I was addicted to everything and absolutely nothing. I reached for anything that would keep me away from being with myself. Whenever a drug dealer asked me, "So what do you want?" I had to think for a second. I went in never knowing what it was I wanted.

Some moments: Standing at the open refrigerator, putting handfuls of shredded cheese into my mouth. Remnants falling through my knuckles onto the kitchen floor. Sneezing and accidentally blowing the powder from the pill all over the car and snorting it anyway. Licking the tops of cd cases that had a tiny bit of powder left. Taking Zantac and Imodium at the same time because I heard the combination got you high. Eating tuna with my fingers out of a container in the fridge. I remember once, while living in a house with roommates, opening the fridge and seeing syringes for their cat's medicine and also narcotics for the dog, and I stood there truly considering using the animals' drugs. I shut the fridge door reluctantly.

My nine-year-old cousin likes to boast, "Eating is my hobby. I love to eat." I cringe, overwhelmed with love for her when I hear her say this—so unselfconscious, so proud. Her little brother Jordan already has a candy addiction. When he wants a piece of gum or candy, he'll hold out his hand and I'll give him one, and he'll always, always, say, "Two." A boy after my own heart. How I fear for him. How does someone learn to take one instead of two?

I watch other people. Their discipline, I mean. I stare. I gape. I've watched people with my jaw dropped while they eat three chips out of the bag and then put the bag on the desk. Maybe they'll eat them later, maybe not. Maybe they'll throw them out. The notion nearly kills me.

In high school, I sometimes bought large bags of Wint O Green Life Savers and ate them all in one sitting. I remember my mom saying, "Imagine all of those mints sitting in your stomach." This has haunted me for years to come. I think of it continually.

"Imagine all of those hydrocodones mixed with alcohol sitting in your stomach."

"Imagine that box of macaroni and cheese sitting in your stomach."

"Imagine those twenty Altoids sitting in your stomach."

"Imagine that bag of marshmallows sitting in your stomach."

Sometimes my interest in eating subsides. Sometimes I binge on health. I pound through Buddhist books by Thich Nhat Hanh and Pema Chödrön. I'll keep a detailed food and exercise journal and feel I've kicked everything. Another verse of "The Swimming Song" goes like this: *This summer I went swimming, this summer I might have drowned. But I held my breath and I kicked my feet and I moved my arms around.*

I never know when I'm going to be triggered and turn right back into that Tic Tac–popping, narcotic-snorting, Yodel-eating girl. I fantasize about being able to buy a pack of mints or chocolate and having it last me over time instead of eating it all in an hour. I fantasize about it. I would like to live out that verse of the song, instead of the self-destructive fool verse, but it's a struggle. I want to kick my feet and move my arms around instead of drown.

"Did you eat dinner?" my dad asked me a few months ago as we drove home from the Albany airport. He saw me look down at the Tic Tacs and he laughed and said, "'Cause I got you some Tic Tacs." They were wintergreen, but I ate a handful anyway.

Hungry Ghost

JUST BEFORE CHRISTMAS a couple of years ago, I made plans with a person whom I deeply admire. I won't say who but I'll say this: she's somewhere on the spectrum between Eileen Myles and Beyoncé. You probably admire her too—or you might hate her and think she's fat. Regardless, she is a Celebrity with a capital C.

I'd been infatuated with the Celebrity and her art for seven years. She was going to come and sleep over at my apartment on a Saturday night. The plans had been in the making for two months, so for two months, I'd been fantasizing about it and preparing for it—posing in the mirror for the photos we would naturally take together. Practicing my smile. The photos would obviously get millions and trillions of likes. My exes would choke on their own spit when they saw. She and I would giggle and eat snacks out of bowls and lie on my newly purchased fifty-dollar futon, spilling our respective guts, the way we both do in our art.

Even then I saw how ridiculous it all was. We'd never met before. She was too famous to take the Amtrak (*I'll take a car, the train can be a little dicey for me*, she'd said). If she was in contact with me, think of the thousands of other people she was in contact with, whom she'd actually met in person. It was the holidays—wouldn't she want to spend these days with her loved ones, her family and her boyfriend, not with me, a stranger? But she'd told me she was free in early December, so I rolled with it.

But how did she know I wasn't a serial killer? A rapist? A sociopath? How did she know I wouldn't have an apartment full of fans just waiting to ask her for favors and take selfies with her? We felt like we knew each other already because of our familiarity with each other's work. This is how I make many of my friends—we've read each other's work, feel like we know each other, and we get drinks. I was used to this pattern, only now the person on the other end happened to be *her*.

The Celebrity was to arrive at noon on Friday. All I'd had to eat since Wednesday were clementines because my stomach was such a mess. I had stress diarrhea. I had an anxiety ball in my chest. At night I dreamed only of her. I had nightmares we were out to dinner and my debit card was declined. I woke early with an energy similar to mania. I took walks and cleaned my apartment, wiping down counters and tables, sweeping floors, driving to T.J. Maxx and walking through the aisles like a zombie, unable to think clearly, buying candles and snacks and towels, considering buying new sheets but also knowing how irrational this was. I caught myself whistling while sweeping—I love whistling—and I remembered my brother noticing this once and telling me that the more people whistle in their lives, the poorer they will be. "Think about farmers," he'd said.

I wanted to give my entire apartment a revamp but couldn't afford to. This was the same apartment I normally boasted about. It is the nicest and most spacious apartment I've had in the entire decade of my twenties. I become enthusiastic when people ask me about it, going so far as to say, *It is the apartment of my dreams.* I say that moving into this apartment was *the best thing that ever happened to me. There are two windows in every single room! There's a closet big enough to write in with a built-in desk and an antique window, look!*

But now I was second guessing, embarrassed about my regular apartment. One minute I was certain she'd be super charmed by the place, it's old and quirky—amazing light, a clawfoot bathtub, maybe she'd want to film here! The next minute I was horrified by the slanting old floors and mismatched bookshelves. I was mortified that I still had a fucking futon. I always thought the first thing I'd do when I finally had money was buy a yellow couch.

• • •

We'd been e-mailing since autumn. She'd read *Women* and publicly supported it. She promoted it on social media and in interviews. On the Amtrak the morning after my book release party in New York City, I was listening to music and staring out the window when I got a notification that she was now following me on Twitter. I'd already been following her for years. She immediately sent me a message telling me she'd loved my book and what could she do to help? She gave me her personal e-mail address and said, *E-mail me anytime.* I began e-mailing her anytime. For every e-mail she wrote, I wrote two or three back.

I called my mom, who accused me of playing an April Fool's Day joke on her, even though it was early October. This was, I thought, many female writers' wet dream. She was like the Oprah of my generation, and I was living my best life. Arrogantly and embarrassingly, I assumed my career was now going to take off in ways I'd never even had the balls to wish for or let myself imagine.

At the beginning of our courtship, we e-mailed about once a week. We e-mailed about different vitamins and herbs we took to stay healthy: oregano oil, probiotics, fish oil. We said we should talk more about vitamins, ideally over smoothies. We e-mailed about books we were reading and wanted to write, about musicians and comedians and writers. She called me "angel" in her e-mails. *We need to meet!* we said. *We are so connected!* we said. We decided that instead of meeting in New York City, she would come to where I lived in Hudson. That way she could get out of the city and enjoy a minivacation, rejuvenate. Should she do a day trip or stay over? we wondered. *I vote sleepover,* she e-mailed. I sent her links of hotels and B&Bs but also said, *Or you can stay at my place.* I admitted I only had a pull-out futon but said it would be an adventure. I was embarrassed, knowing she was used to high-end hotels. I knew it would probably be fine, she didn't expect me to be a millionaire, but I could not shake the voice of shame.

"Chloe thinks she's e-mailing once a week with *you-know-who,*" my friend Elizabeth joked. "But she's probably just getting catfished."

I was cautious about telling *everyone*, but I told a healthy handful of people. I asked for advice. My mom told me to cut up fruit. *If you cut it up and peel it, people will eat it*, she texted, seeming as stressed as I was. My friend Fran told me if she were in Hudson, she would cook beef bourguignon. My friend Amanda asked if she could crash our dinner. My friend Ana said if we wanted to go to Hanukkah at her house, we could. Middle-aged women in my small town told me to bring her over for tea. My brother made a point, saying, "Have they ever invited you over for tea by yourself?"

Fran's comment about the beef bourguignon bothered me. Not because she said it, but because I began to beat myself up for not being able to cook. It would be so cozy to convene in my kitchen with music and wine. How I wished more than anything I could cook beef bourguignon.

Thankfully, though, she and I planned on having cheeseburgers. She was public and shameless about also not knowing how to cook. I'd read interviews and heard podcasts where she spoke of it. She'd e-mailed me that cheeseburgers were her passion, trumped only by hot dogs. We would go out for burgers. I had two restaurants in mind.

I see now I wanted to be seen with her. Being seen, this was the seed of my life. A writer friend who is a practicing therapist as well once told me this is why writers write. They don't feel seen. I think this must apply to the Celebrity and me both. When we walked to get burgers, would we be stopped on the street?

It's true she and I were connected in many ways. We saw eye to eye on feminism, we crafted our life experiences into hyper-personal and sometimes provocative art. My first book—a collection of personal essays—was compared half a dozen times to her and/or her work in reviews. I am not into celebrity gossip and spent years not knowing names of the most famous actors and actresses. But this woman was different. Looking at her, a woman whose birthday was a month after mine (yep, I knew when her birthday was) was like looking into the mirror and seeing a more successful version of myself.

Just over the summer, an acquaintance from high school had asked me if I'd ever met her.

"No!" I said defensively. "How and why would I have met her?"

"You meet a lot of people, and you guys write similar stuff." She shrugged.

I was flattered by this, but it also made me panic. I'd felt so strongly about her work for years. She was the one artist I would want to meet, if I could meet anyone. I did not dare fantasize about meeting her even in the secret recesses of my own brain, because the devastation I would feel when I didn't would break my heart. It was too far-fetched. Which made this attention from her all the more surreal.

◆ ◆ ◆

Besides the cheeseburgers, I didn't make other plans. Perhaps I should have, but I could barely think that far ahead, and I get off on winging things. I tried to imagine us chatting in my living room and kitchen, maybe watching a TV show or a movie. I imagined a lot of laughter and selfies.

Things I bought in preparation:

Salami roll
Three candles
· lavender
· plain, unscented
· honeysuckle
Two kinds of cheese
· Goat Brie
· Comté
A puce-green mug that read You're an Amazing Woman in a tacky font from T.J. Maxx, as a half joke (I was torn on the mug and texted a photo to Karina and asked her opinion. *She'll love that! It's the perfect amount of creepy*, she responded.)

Chocolate-covered almonds
Three kinds of crackers (including, obviously, the trendy
    Mary's gluten-free kind)
Baguette
Arugula

T.J. Maxx—this is where I did my shopping. Where I live, your
choices are either high-as-fuck-end or T.J. Maxx and Walmart. I
went to T.J. Maxx for the candles and the almonds and crackers
and a pretentious cheese shop in town for the cheese and salami.
I thought if I mixed shabby and fancy, no one would notice.

"What the fuck is a salami roll?" Fran later asked me. "I get
that shit sliced," she said.

I knew the Celebrity didn't drink much, so I got something
pink with low alcohol content. I'd gone into the wine store and
said excitedly, "I have a girl friend coming this weekend and
want to get some nice champagne." When I look back on this
moment, I feel totally pathetic. Overambitious and caught up
in my own story.

In Buddhism, the term *hungry ghost* refers to the person whose
appetite exceeds their capacity for satisfaction. The visual of a
hungry ghost is a Buddha-ghost with a tiny mouth and an enormous stomach. They're greedy, starved for money, sex, drugs,
power, status, all the good stuff. More is never enough. Though I've
done my fair share of self-work—therapy, books, yoga teacher training, meditation—I have hungry ghost tendencies I must keep in
check. When I started what I thought would be this epic friendship with the Celebrity, I really did want to be close and intimate
with her, but my hungry ghost started haunting my dreams, surprising even me.

I was anxious over what to wear before settling on all black.
It was the safest. I was working at a boutique where plain black
shirts cost seventy-five dollars. Desperate, I asked my boss if she
could take it out of my paycheck. *Sorry I'm acting insane,* I texted her, and told her who was coming to sleep over. OH MY GOD

GOTCHA!!!!! she wrote back, and then: *Bring her into the store this weekend to shop!*

.   .   .

"I'm obsessed with money. I eat, sleep, and breathe it," I told my therapist.

She chuckled.

"What?" I asked.

"You said the same thing last week."

"Well, it's gotten worse."

I wasn't exaggerating. I walked around with headphones in my ears and, depending on whether my mood was optimistic or pessimistic, I'd sing along with Lana Del Rey, *I want money, power, and glory,* or *It's not about the money, money, money, we don't need your money, money, money, wanna make the world dance, forget about your price tag* by Jessie J.

I'd recently noticed I talked about money and income differently than other people. I was constantly mentioning if I'd received a check I'd been waiting on or if I was still waiting for checks. I greeted people with "I got my check" or listed the checks I would be receiving in the following weeks. No one told me about their checks or asked me about mine, but I couldn't stop offering this information, like a nervous tic.

I did not tell my therapist the Celebrity was coming to sleep over, for a few reasons. I thought I would sound grandiose. And if the Celebrity canceled, I'd be humiliated. Also, I didn't want to jinx it.

I planned on giving the Celebrity the Amazing Woman mug and a book called *The Writer on Her Work,* even though that book meant a lot to me and had been a gift from my mother for my twenty-second birthday. The book was a compilation of essays by classic and contemporary women writers on their personal lives and craft. It was a hardcover. It was a beautiful and special book, and I'd never seen it anywhere else. I would let her believe I bought it, that I picked it out especially for her.

I don't have a guest room. I would give her my bedroom, I decided, and I would sleep on the futon in the living room. I didn't have a real couch. I didn't have a TV. I didn't have a coffee table. I didn't have my own apartment—I had one roommate. Luckily, she was mellow and kind, often at work, and not one bit concerned about a guest occupying our space for a night.

I'll admit, my active imagination went full force, and I did imagine sleeping and cuddling in my bed together.

What would it be like brushing our teeth together? If she forgot her toothbrush, would she use mine? Would she think I was lame if I had Crest toothpaste and not Tom's, the natural kind? Would we change into our pajamas in the same room? What if we ran out of subjects to talk about? What if someone had to poop in the morning and the other person could hear? Smell? Karina told me she was surprised about my nerves.

"You're normally so relaxed about meeting famous writers and stuff," she said.

I guess I understood what she meant. I'd met many writers of high caliber and developed friendships with some of them. Through writing, I've become very close to Cheryl Strayed. I've often slept at her house and babysat her kids. We've seen each other in our pajama pants in the six-thirty a.m. light, I euthanized her cat, I broke one of her SodaStream bottles, and once I even clogged her toilet.

But the Celebrity was not a famous writer. She was a *celebrity*. Cheryl's fame came to her in her forties, but the Celebrity and I are exactly the same age. Plus, I'd met Cheryl before *Wild*—now a national best seller and mainstream movie—had been released. She had much more time back then, time to write me long, heartfelt e-mails, and I remember once seeing her tweeting at Tillamook Cheese.

"I can't believe you're imagining brushing your teeth together," Karina said.

"*Of course* I am!" I retorted.

"I bet she's hyper," Fran said.

I kept trying to forget the hard, cold fact that the Celebrity is a millionaire. Perhaps you've figured this out by now, but I am not a millionaire. I got nothing for my first book, and three thousand dollars for my second, which was the most money I'd ever seen or earned in my life. But I felt excited that we both seemed to be highly evolved with this. She knows I know she's a millionaire, and I know she knows I am not. But I still felt shame, wished I had nicer furniture and clothing, wished I was a more success-ful author, wished I came from a more comfortable upbringing. I don't think she knew how little I had. I didn't know what her expectations were for my apartment or for this experience. My friends reassured me she must have other broke artist friends, and she probably needs good girl friends at this point in her career.

Sometimes people assume since I have two books out, I have more money than I do. That I'm getting cut healthy royalty checks. When my name suddenly was linked with hers by crit-ics and national publications, people's perception of me changed. Acquaintances I run into (not writers—writers know) at the local Mexican restaurant say, "You're doing really well, how does it feel?" with knowing looks. It's a difficult question to answer. The people asking always seem happy for me, their eyes look into mine, and they truly believe, because they saw some press some-where online or in a local paper, I'm living comfortably.

I am not living comfortably. I have never received a royalty check. My mom sometimes gives me Price Chopper gift cards with twenty-five dollars on them. I eat eggs and oatmeal and lentils and frozen bananas and peanut butter sandwiches. I put a bunch of salt and pepper on the eggs to make for a more satisfying meal, a trick my brother taught me when we lived together in Brooklyn. I read books with money tips, like taking the thin paper that separates fruit at the grocery store home for toilet paper. I keep a money journal. At the end of each evening, I jot down what I have purchased, then label it *bad* or *good* or *luxury!* On the best days, I have spent zero dollars, and then I draw a smiley face. I often go into my mom's or dad's house with a backpack when they're not home to steal necessities—I leave with an extra roll of toilet paper, some tea, a can of black beans, and a box of pasta I'm sure they won't miss.

Nothing I buy during this time in my life is purchased without panic, a raised heartbeat, guilt, shame, worry, existentialism. Not because I am responsible, but because I am seriously broke. Not broke like I have a savings account with five hundred dollars for emergencies. There is no savings account. There is no car. There is no credit card. There is no "real" job. There is no backup plan, only rice and beans and cans of tuna. I was sweeping the floor. I was changing my sheets. I was wondering if I should buy *new* sheets. Wondering if I should put a mint on her pillow. I was buying $3.99 candles at T.J. Maxx on the verge of overdrafting my checking account.

◆ ◆ ◆

I decided I'd wear the new black Three Dots shirt that my boss was taking out of my paycheck, black Levis, and my black No. 6 clogs, which are the most expensive thing I've ever owned, an impulse credit card purchase after seeing Ingmar Bergman's *Scenes from a Marriage* in play form at the New York Theater Workshop in the East Village with Fran (her treat).

I suspected she would arrive wearing a fabulous vintage fur coat and some graphic ironic sweatshirt. I would feel like a plain Jane, a feeling I loathe, but I believed this would be the safest option. I'd just make my hair look good and wear makeup.

Karina declared this sleepover meeting to be a moment in history. "It's like Dylan and Hendrix meeting," she said. "Like Taylor Swift and Karlie Kloss. Like Patti Smith and Eileen Myles." This was not a comfort to me at all.

Fran eventually decided she was going to fly all the way from Portland to New York to help me and have dinner with us. She knew I needed her. She was about to purchase her ticket, and at the last minute her son came down with a wretched flu.

◆ ◆ ◆

On the deepest level in my gut, I knew she was not coming. How could she come? It was ridiculous. Idealistic. Flighty. Fantasy.

But she'd told me she'd gotten a driver, and she would leave the city around ten a.m. I had to take her at her word. Though I'd possibly be cooler, more authentic, if I didn't scrub the toilet and change my books around so the obscure ones would show.

Just a friendly reminder that the Celebrity is coming to sleep over at your house tomorrow, my friend Erika texted me the night before she was supposed to arrive.

This day was particularly hard. I swept and vacuumed and burned sage in each room. My roommate suggested I take a long walk to burn off some of my energy. Good idea. I went off, headphones in my ears. My phone rang; it was Karina, who was at JFK airport. I told her how out of control I was feeling, how bizarre I thought the whole situation was. How did my life bring me to this point, this situation? When we hung up, I went to do my final errands (arugula, cheese, champagne, laundry), and then I went to work at the boutique, grateful I had something to occupy these hours.

When I got home from the boutique at six p.m., I sat down at my desk. Like clockwork, an e-mail from her popped in.

Sending more love and more disappointment. In the meantime, should we Skype? (: she wrote.

Huh? O.K., this was a weird cancellation. And the smiley face at the end pissed me off. My heart sank. It was a strange feeling— since I had predicted this, I couldn't be shocked. But I was still profoundly disappointed and a touch humiliated. I read the e-mail to my roommate and she was like, "Where's the rest of it?" That's the whole e-mail, I told her. I forwarded it to everyone I'd told, saying, *I knew it.* The truth was, I felt enormous relief.

My mom called me. "Are you O.K.?"

Fran called me. "Are you O.K.?" she asked.

"How fucked up was that?" she asked.

"Where does it say she's not coming?" my brother asked.

After the cancellation, my jaw relaxed. I'd been clenching it. My shoulders relaxed. I hadn't been sleeping well and fatigue set in. My appetite slowly came back. I was mortified at the food and candles I'd bought. They looked ridiculous in my kitchen. A twelve-dollar salami roll? Cheese that cost as much as a new hardcover book? This purple smelly candle? Who do I think I am?

"At least you didn't buy new sheets," Fran said.

My younger cousin Sam had e-mailed me the previous day. He went to college in Montreal and was coming to New York for his holiday break. He was getting a ride with friends, could they drop him at my place? We could hang out? *Not really*, I'd told him. *I'm going to have a famous person from the city here, and I don't want to bombard her.*

What a dick. So now I messaged him. *Yes, come! She canceled! I have wine and champagne and cheese.* He responded, *Say no more.*

God bless this timing. I imagine I'd have otherwise cracked the wine, binge eaten cheese, cried into my pillow, perhaps smashed one of the candles, texted an ex.

My "the-Oprah-of-our-generation-is-coming" outfit morphed into my "my-cousin-is-coming-from-Montreal" outfit. I made a cheese and meat plate.

I chilled the champagne. I lit my new T.J. Maxx candles. I decided to give Sam the *BOMB* magazine I'd set on my coffee table to look cool as a Christmas gift.

My tall cousin and his tall college friends showed up at my door. This is such a cool apartment, they said. It smells so good in here, they said. Can we use the washroom—we call it "the washroom" in Canada, they said. Sorry for the weird question, but is that a tongue scraper in your bathroom? they asked. Sam and I opened the wine. He plowed through the salami roll.

"I'm so glad you're eating that!" I exclaimed. "I only bought it because I thought the Celebrity was going to be here today."

My cousin obviously didn't share my bewilderment. He shrugged. He was in his final year of college and had more serious matters on his mind.

His dad—my uncle—arrived, bottle of red wine in hand. My mom and her husband brought over a pot of chili and a baguette, and more wine. My aunt and uncle surprised us by coming down to visit from a few hours further north, saying that morning they decided they wanted to be spontaneous, and brought more wine. My brother showed up. My dad rang the doorbell. We got rowdy, we got drunk, we smoked weed, we killed the pot of chili, seven wine bottles in the recycling. We pretended we were on the show *Parenthood*. We walked to a bar and danced. The chili was the first warm meal I'd eaten in what felt like weeks. I felt loved and like I was with exactly whom I was supposed to be with. I was humbled. I opened the chocolate-covered almonds from T.J. Maxx and was instantly even more relieved she hadn't come. They tasted and smelled like plastic. They were old. Stale. Imagine if she had busted her tooth on one of them.

. . .

Shortly after the cancellation, my dad and I drove to a movie. He felt sorry for me because he knew how excited I'd been about her coming over. (*Are you very close with your dad?* she'd asked. *I'm sort of obsessed with mine.*)

"It's not exactly the same," my dad offered, "but it kind of reminds me of when people at my music store tell me they're going to buy the kid-sized drum set, and then I never hear from them again."

"Yeah," I said, stifling my laughter. "It's kind of like that."

My dad also told me he'd secretly thought this was a really brave thing for her to do—plan a sleepover with someone she'd never met.

"Maybe she was excited about you and your book at first, but then it faded," he said.

. . .

Weeks later, the Celebrity and I figured out I hadn't been getting her e-mails. Gmail at some point had prompted me to create a "Google name," and I didn't do it, so they assigned me one:

myemailaddress1. This meant when I e-mailed people, my e-mails didn't come from Chloe Caldwell; they said "myemailadress1" in the "from" field. So people thought my e-mail address had the number one after it, which it doesn't. Turned out the Celebrity had sent me a long cancellation e-mail full of remorse and kind words to myemailaddress1@gmail.com. I never got the e-mail until a month later. I was relieved, because I'd been thinking maybe she was an asshole. After this mishap, I changed my Google name to my actual name.

We did meet, after all, in New York City. She invited me to an upscale party, a premiere for something or other. I didn't have money for the Amtrak, and my mom generously bought my train tickets and gave me money to get my hair blown out. Riding on the train that day, it was clear to me that if my parents were dead, I wouldn't have been able to go to this event.

I got a plus one with my invitation and brought Karina. I figured Karina would be a good date because she is good at talking to people. She holds alcohol well and stays way more lucid than I do. She doesn't seem to have social anxiety and likes staying out late. Both in black dresses, we walked into the party, a formal-dress event with multiple open bars, "charge your iPhone" stations, and "get your makeup touched up" stations.

Karina and I stood on the balcony in silence for a minute, staring and overwhelmed. There were recognizable celebrities everywhere. I worried Karina would want to leave early, or she would get anxious and talk about how we didn't belong. In the cab earlier, she'd mentioned some friends who wanted to meet up with us, after. "After?" I said. I doubted there would be an after—I planned to stay in this room as long as I possibly could. It might be the one and only time I attended something like this, and I planned on milking it.

I swear, it's like we had an unspoken agreement there on the stairs: *Let's do this.* Next thing you know, we were chatting with Abbi Jacobson and Ilana Glazer of *Broad City* (who backed away from me slowly as I eagerly stepped toward them but then complimented

me on my necklace), and we all joked about the movie *Corrina,
Corrina*. Then Gaby Hoffman asked Karina if she would snap
a photo of her with a friend. As the night went on, we got ball-
sier, swooping in to talk to more people. We pretended we were
comfortable and we belonged; therefore we were comfortable and
belonged. *Besides,* I thought, *how do these people know I'm not a
TV or film writer?* Whenever I introduced myself as a writer, I
would be asked, "For what show?" I was tempted to lie.

We drank countless cocktails, ate salad and steak, and got our
lipstick done at the L'Oréal station, where the woman told me I
looked like Christina Applegate. She gave us free eyeliner we hap-
pily put in our purses. We made rounds, used the photo station,
ran into a writer and an agent we knew, had what felt like deep and
charged conversations about getting older; our arms were getting
harder to get back into shape, and spider veins were showing up.
The hours flew by while I felt no concept of time passing.

Later Karina admitted she'd imagined the event at a bougie
dive bar with couches and candles. She could not have been further off.

The Celebrity, the only reason we were there, was so inun-
dated with people she didn't move from where she was standing the entire night. Karina and I got to explore and drink and
people-watch and eat. It's more fun to be a nonfamous person at
these kinds of events. Toward the end of the night, I finally saw
her and she saw me.

We hugged sweetly, and she whispered, "I feel so connected to
you." I told her she'd been an extremely important artist to me for
a long time. We laughed over the missed e-mails. "I'm sorry you
didn't get my apology e-mail and thought I was such a douche,"
she said. "I could *tell* you didn't get it! Can you believe I remembered to follow up?" she asked. "I'm going to write you a long
e-mail tomorrow," she said. "I feel like we're real friends," she said.
And then she was talking to the next person, and we were waving
good-bye.

After the Celebrity and I spoke, Karina said, "She yelled
your name." When I find myself telling this story to others, I

almost always incorporate this detail. "She yelled my *name*," I say emphatically.

We were some of the last people to leave the party. Gaby Hoffman's heels were off by that point, and Karina accidentally stepped on her bare foot; Gaby told her not to worry about it.

Karina and I took a cab to Kellogg's Diner in Williamsburg because after the black-tie event and hors d'oeuvres and heels that were now killing our feet, we had to take it back to our level. We ordered cheeseburgers and fries and Budweisers. Separately, we each went to the bathroom and came out mortified. We had lipstick around the outsides of our mouths. We looked drunk. "Why didn't you tell me I looked like this?" we both asked each other. We laughed about it and took a cab back to Karina's in Bed-Stuy, where I slept in my thong and fishnets on her couch. I woke up sick and thirsty but elated. Snow was falling. I walked to the subway and then to Penn Station. I had to get back home to work at the boutique.

Christmas came around, and I gave the Amazing Woman mug to Karina, who rolled her eyes, knowing it wasn't originally intended for her. When I see the Celebrity in the news now, I still imagine brushing our teeth together. I haven't given up that dream. Karina left New York City six months later, and I saw the puce-green mug packed in her suitcase. Six months after *that*, she texted one morning to say she had a nightmare. In it, the mug broke into a million pieces.

◆   ◆   ◆

After the New Year, I received another e-mail from the Celebrity. She said she thinks about our e-mail courtship often. She said she still wants to come visit, bad. I respond, but don't acknowledge that part. I could never survive that internal drama again, no matter how amazing of a woman she is. Like many of my exes and ex-friends, she's turned into somewhat of a ghost—someone who occasionally "likes" one of my Instagram photos; and every couple of months I'll wake up to an e-mail from her that she sent after midnight.

The Writer on Her Work continued to sit expectantly in its gift bag on a shelf in my room through February. The purple ribbon drooped in its bow. I woke up in the morning, stared at it from my bed. The icicles hanging outside my window were starting to melt. I groggily walked over to the bag, untied the ribbon, put the gift bag in the recycling, and put my book back on my shelf where it belonged.

PART 2

Soul Killer

I GOT A PEDICURE EACH TIME I promised myself I'd stop doing heroin—which is to say, I got pedicures that whole summer. Pedicures gave me the false notion I was about to get my shit together. I wasn't functioning well—my brain cells were spent, and my serotonin was depleted. Sitting despondent in a vinyl chair was as good as it got.

My acne had taken over any joy in my life, and I was routinely suffering through opiate withdrawal, so I'd go to the nail salon in the middle of the day when it was quiet and I could avoid seeing humans. I liked eating the candy from the candy bowl. I took handfuls of Dum Dums, peppermints, butterscotch, and those strawberry candies with the gooey middle grandmothers always have in little dishes in their houses. I sat in the massage chair, crunched down loudly on my candies, and watched Lifetime movies with subtitles. I pushed buttons on the remote to control the strength of the massage, and I drifted in and out of half-sleep.

I hated myself. I actually hated myself. I never got manicures. They would be too much work, sitting upright and making small talk. Plus, I bite my fingernails so badly they can't be manicured. A disgusting addiction, but in comparison with my other addictions, I let it slide. I have too many battles to fight with myself, so I choose them carefully.

In June, after one of my pedicures, I left the nail salon and got into the car. I don't say *my* car, because I shared it with my dad. I was living with my dad at the time, and we shared everything—the bathroom, food; we even worked together at his music store. The car was an eggplant-colored PT Cruiser. I checked my phone. My mom had left me a voice mail asking me

to go on a hike with her before she left for Costa Rica. I would
have rather done anything than go on a hike, but I drove to meet
her instead of starting a fight. I was wearing flip-flops because I
didn't want to ruin my pedicure. As we hiked, I couldn't speak.
My jaw was locked. *Mom. Mom. Mom. Help me*, I thought. *Please
help me.*

My mom knew I was depressed, but she didn't know why. We
sat on a log when we reached the top of the hill. Sometimes all
my mother has to do is touch me the right way or say the right
sensitive thing, and I'll tell her anything. She was doing those
things, saying, "What is it?" but I knew I couldn't burden her
with this. Tears streamed down my face. She put her arm around
me, and we sat on the log for a long time. "Wow, did you just get
your feet done? They look beautiful," she said. When we parted
ways I told myself that was it. No more heroin. I drove away from
the woods in my flip-flops, listening to mainstream rap on the
radio. The color of the toenail polish I'd chosen was called Cha-
Ching Cherry.

The cycle went like this: The worse my skin got, the more
stressed I felt and the more heroin I would buy. The more heroin I
snorted, the worse my skin would get and the more stressed I would
become. I couldn't find the source of my sadness, my stress, or my
acne. Each was feeding the others.

Through my adolescence and teens, my skin was clear. I didn't
have one blemish. I was like Snow White: pale, with soft skin
and a round face. My friend Julie had the same complexion as
me. "Ghosts!" the boys would call as we walked by. Because of
this, we went tanning after school every day. My skin was fake
bronzed and glowing. Julie's skin may have been whiter than
mine—she recently told me it was so white it was blue. We cov-
ered up our insecurities with red lipstick and Sun-In. We didn't
know how lucky we were. I didn't have Noxzema or Proactiv or
Retin-A because I did not need them. Until I did.

I moved to New York City shortly after my twentieth birthday—acne-free and a recreational drug user depending on whom
I was around or what I was offered. Julie went away to college.

Around twenty-two or twenty-three, I started having minor breakouts. I thought it was a fluke. I thought I was having a weird week. Then I thought I was having a weird couple of months. I went into denial. I wasn't going to have a problem with acne because I wasn't a person who got acne. We are attached to ideas about ourselves. If I'd just accepted the acne, I could have possibly prevented it from getting as bad as it did.

I've used drugs to numb myself since I was sixteen. They've helped me be there but not really *there*. When my parents separated, I found weed. When the man I loved didn't love me back enough, I drank myself silly and snorted cocaine. After a bad car accident, I fell into the painkiller sinkhole. Opiates were my solution to my acne problem. Got a bunch of zits? Buy a bag of heroin. Depressed about how you look? Text your drug dealer. What else was there to do? I read a comment on xoJane once:

Fuck acne! It's evil. It has literally made me forget who I am as a person.

Precisely.

After years of roaming and railing, at twenty-five, I began living with my dad in upstate New York. My dad stood in line with me at cvs after my first dermatologist appointment. I cried. My prescription for Differin was something like 175 dollars. My dad looked scared of my sadness. We went out to breakfast, carrying the prescription bags of expensive acne products that wouldn't work. It was a French café, and there were mirrors on the walls. I sat in the booth, facing away from the mirror. I'd rather rub my own piss on my face (which I did, years later—it's an acne-calming tactic) than look in a mirror. My dad pointed out the mirrors.

"I never noticed the mirrors in here," he said.

"I know," I said. "Why do you think I'm sitting on *this* side?"

"I became expert at learning what mirrors would soften the effect," David Shields writes in *The Thing About Life Is That One Day You'll Be Dead*. Same. I would not go to certain restaurants (diners in the morning), and I would not make eye contact with myself in cheap motel bathrooms while I brushed my teeth (fluorescent lights).

I would not have chosen to have my heroin phase while I was living under my father's roof, but we don't always decide when certain drugs come into our lives—same goes for people.

The thing about my heroin experience is I did heroin when I did the most mundane tasks. I snorted heroin and went to the Dollar General. I went to Stop & Shop and bought yogurt. I treated my acne. I changed my profile picture. I updated my status. I cleaned my room. I went to bed. I wasn't out partying. I was home in bed on the computer reading acne forums. When you stay in your bedroom and have heroin, you're a king. You can be checking your e-mail and be a king, eating an apple. Your world becomes quite small.

Julie graduated college in California and moved back upstate. We've known each other since age seven—ever since we ran through her neighbor's woods, resulting in poison ivy. She's the kind of friend who calls and you both immediately launch into who you slept with, how you feel, how depressed you are, what mental illness you think you have. "If I have it—you have it!" we like to yell at each other. "Oh, I don't have it," the other will say with a smile. Later, after some drinks or heroin, your friend will come around and say, "You were right before. I *have* always thought I have histrionic borderline personality disorder."

Julie was hilarious, with great bone structure and long black hair. She was intimidating in her beauty and her blunt way of speaking, and people were scared of her. Some hated her, during high school and after. Acne hit her too. Our acne overlapped. While she was in college and I was bouncing around various cities, her text messages to me consisted of miserable photos of her face. We texted products back and forth—so hopeful we'd finally found the answer. *You gotta buy this!* we'd text, with a photo of tea tree soap or Dr. Bronner's or Clarisonic exfoliating pads.

Julie understood when I cried about my skin, and she would hug me through the window of the car and say, "I know, I know. Lie in the sun. Take a shower. Don't pick at it. Here, have the rest of my heroin." Our relationship was precarious. My mother thought she was a bad influence on me, and her mother thought I was a bad influence on her. We'd begin our summer evenings by walking around in the sun, complaining about how small our town was. Then we'd go for a beer. Then tequila shots. We waited for the other to say, "We should get shit. We should text B." Someone always said it. The other one always agreed. We wanted each other to feel good. We loved each other—but we loved ourselves more. We stayed out all night talking about monogamy, men, women, mothers. Did we want to have children? Would we rather be fat or have acne? Did we want to get clean? We got riled up. We cried and laughed uncontrollably. And we went to the bathroom to do lines together. Julie usually puked. She had a weak stomach. In the afternoon, she'd call me around three p.m. after she'd woken up. We giggled and giggled into the phone about our antics, not needing to speak any words. Sometimes I went alone to buy drugs, but usually we were together. Julie once removed her toenail polish and repainted her toes while sitting shotgun in the car.

My acne was so bad I couldn't sleep on one side of my face. I couldn't smile or chew. I couldn't go to work. I couldn't see myself or remember who I was aside from my face. When I'd visit various dermatologists, they'd ask if I had the acne anywhere else. My back? My neck? I wish, I'd tell them. I wished for back acne so badly. Alas, my back was clear as can be. It was my face, the first thing people saw, that was fucked.

"Remember," my mom would say, "*you* are not the pimple or the cyst. It's just one thing about you, not who you are." True, but acne makes you feel desperate. Heroin makes you feel beautiful. They went hand in hand.

At my best, I'd have a day or two of clear-ish skin. Once I was lucky enough for this to coincide with a day I had to do a reading in New York City. Like an alcoholic, I didn't only do heroin when I was down. I did it when I was up. That morning I bought three decks of heroin and shoved them in my jeans. I did some in the train bathroom. As the train pulled into Penn Station, my phone vibrated. It was my ex-boyfriend Simon, the one it took me three years and three cities to get over. He was saying hi. Letting me know he'd love to see me, if I ever came to the city.

Obviously, I could have ignored the text. But he caught me on a clear-skin day and a holding-heroin day. I could hang out with him but have my secret friend, my scapegoat, my false confidence. I pondered this while I walked into Urban Outfitters. It was also good-body-image day. I couldn't control my face, but at least I could control my body. I tried on some sexy dresses. It was June and hot. I bought a bright-blue sundress with spaghetti straps that showed off my cleavage. I poured some heroin out of the baggie onto my cell phone in the dressing room, looking myself in the eye, smiling. Then I texted him back. *I'm actually here now. Do you want to meet me at the Strand?*

We met up and sat in Union Square. We had drinks at a bar neither of us had been to before. It was too early and too hot for red wine, but I loved red wine with heroin, so I got a glass anyway. I went to the bathroom twice to snort more. I was honest with him about my struggles—we'd always been super close. I said I'd been partying pretty hard. He said, "Well, you don't look like it. You look really good. Healthy." And there it was—the ability to appear one thing and to be another.

We walked to my reading and drank there for a few hours. Readings were events I liked to be high for, and I suppose this was because the book I was reading from was incredibly exposing and vulnerable; therefore, I needed a shield of protection. When I think back to this time, all I see are bathrooms. I was always changing clothes or using makeup or snorting lines. At the reading, I went into the bathroom and changed from my new Urban Outfitters dress to a slinky black sequined dress.

"You went into the bathroom already looking awesome and came out looking like Superwoman!" Simon exclaimed.

Never one to keep much to myself, when we finally got to Simon's apartment, I came clean. His response: "Can I do a line?"

We had sloppy sex all night—neither of us could come. I remember brushing my hair a lot because it felt really good. In the morning, I had to sneak out of bed early and put makeup on so he wouldn't see my real face. We got bagels, hung out on the roof of a building he liked, and talked. He told me he didn't like heroin. He liked coke better.

"Be careful with your drugs," he said, before shutting his apartment door. "You can't write when you're dead."

I caught my train and headed back upstate high on anxiety, curling into the fetal position on my seat. The next day, I broke out with cysts all over my face. "Why do we do these things? Why do we go backwards?" I asked my friend Sean. "We do them to remember why we don't do them," he said.

I read an article called "Why Acne Psychologist Dr. Ted Grossbart Blames My Ex for My Bad Skin." He says: "Your skin as a loyal part of your mind/body complex, may well be saying, 'Hey, we need to protect her from getting hurt.'"

"Do you ever think that you and Julie have bad skin now because of . . . karma?" my friend Amy asked me. She had a point. Julie and I were bitches in high school.

Buddhists say anger causes acne. And I was angry—angry at myself. Where was my character? Where was my discipline? Who was I? Wasn't I better than this? And yet, I could not stop. I dreaded when my dad would ask me to run an errand—because each time I got into the PT Cruiser, I'd drive to my dealer's block. *Hey*, I'd text. *Hey girl, how many slices?* he'd ask. My usual was two. They were tiny wax bags with a red or black stamp on them. They had different names. "Fire" was one. "Apple" was another. And then—I kid you not—there was "Soul Killer."

Was it anger or was it my karma? Was it my hormones or was it my genes? Should I cut out meat or should I cut out dairy? Was I allergic to gluten? Was it my ex or was it my stress level? No one knew. And yet everyone had an opinion. I was enraged, frustrated, mortified, and heartbroken.

"I want to kill someone!" was my mantra, and I loved yelling it. "I want to kill someone." "I don't think you want to kill someone," my dad tried to reason with me. "I do! I do, Dad! I really would love to. I want to kill someone." That morning, I slammed my fist into the wall like a fourteen-year-old boy. My father was shocked, as was I. But I wasn't in control anymore. I stomped into the bathroom and slammed the door behind me.

I stepped into the dreaded shower. I hated taking showers and using my dumb products that weren't working, I hated feeling the bumps on my face, but I mostly hated stepping out and having to look at myself in the mirror without makeup. And putting makeup on sucked too. Mornings were the worst. I looked like I had been hit by a truck. It took me forever to make myself look even a little less dead. My dad kept telling me he wished he could take it on for me, that he would if he could. It choked me up whenever he said this. I wished he could too.

My having acne changed my dad's perspective on how he dealt with some of the teenagers he gave guitar lessons to. "Sometimes I think, *Should I be extra nice to you, just because you have acne?*" he told me about one of his students. Sometimes while I worked at the store, I had to hold a hot compress on my cysts at the same time.

There's an essay on Jezebel about cystic acne that says, "Fighting acne is like fighting a war. There is collateral damage. Things get worse before they get better."

Things got worse. At my lowest, I was my highest. In early December, Julie, Amy, and I drove to New York City. I was battling a stubborn cyst on the side of my face, but besides that, my skin was decent. I gave a reading at Happy Ending Lounge on Bowery Street, and Julie put makeup on my cyst before I read. I'd invited my friend William, a functioning heroin addict. He slipped me two hot-pink baggies. Julie and I went into the bathroom. And we came out way happier. This was nothing like the stuff we got upstate. This was the real deal. We had grand fun that night—that I know—but I don't remember much. But I felt good. On the way home, Julie and I ate a bag of Tate's chocolate chip cookies, our favorite.

Our friend dropped Julie and me off at my house late at four a.m. We fell into my bed and snuggled into each other. Around five thirty a.m., Julie and I both jumped up, like we heard it at the same time. My father was on the phone. He was talking about us. He was defending us. Defending me. He was saying I wasn't doing drugs. Julie and I got out of bed and put our ears to the door. I heard him say he agreed that Julie and I should be better friends and examples to each other. We looked at each other with shocked eyes. Eventually we opened the door.

My dad hung up. He was pissed.

My father was kind but stern. He said, "But if you're doing heroin—I want you to cut the shit. I have a short rope for that. My brother died from it. Just—stop."

"We're not!" we told him. "We're not."

I remembered my father's brother. He was my favorite uncle when I was a kid. He was always dozing off in a recliner. He ate Cocoa Puffs and drank Sunny D. He was laid-back and there, but not really *there*. I was with my father at Uncle's funeral. I was twelve. I'd never seen my dad cry before. I laid my head on his shoulder. I always told my dad Uncle Steve reminded me of Will Smith's character in *The Fresh Prince of Bel-Air*. My dad loved that story. He often asked me to repeat it.

I wondered if my dad 100 percent believed Julie and me. I really just wished someone would ask me point blank if I was o.k. so I could say no. Even I could see my behavior was erratic. I was either sleeping ten hours a night or not sleeping at all. I was either binge eating or not eating at all. The sky was always falling. I was always pissed about something. Everyone was an asshole. I loved to bitch about how annoying everyone was.

When I woke up in the mornings, I would find comments I wrote online I did not remember writing. I sent naked photographs I did not remember sending. My wallet was full of empty heroin wrappers. I flushed them down the toilet when I remembered, but usually I forgot. I wasn't exactly organized. Sometimes when I was paying for gas or gum or something, I'd reach into the change pocket and feel all the little baggies, reminding me of my other self, my second life, my alter ego.

I watched videos of Cassandra Bankson to comfort myself. Cassandra Bankson is a model who was born in 1992. She, like me, had severe cystic acne. On her YouTube channel, she posts videos of her struggles with acne. Sometimes my dad watched them with me. One video begins showing her with makeup on, then she washes it off. She shows her acne to the camera. She says, "This is my biggest insecurity." There are trillions of cool and bizarre anomalies on the internet, but this is the coolest one. With makeup on, she looks like the supermodel that she is. When she wipes it off, her acne is the worst I've ever seen on anyone—worse than my own. One night when my cousin Megan was visiting, we stayed up past midnight in my bed watching videos of Cassandra. I couldn't believe what my life had turned into: living at home at twenty-six years old, still having sleepovers, watching acne videos.

I was eating only certain foods—mainly Dannon Light & Fit pineapple coconut yogurt. You could pretty much taste the chemicals; there must have been something really, really bad for you in it. I craved milk and dairy. I became tiny. I was in my sixteen-year-old body. "You gonna eat something?" a guy at the coffee shop I went to started saying, flirtatiously.

"I bet you weigh what you weighed in high school," Julie said one night when we were hanging out in my room trying on dresses. "You look like a completely different person from the back than you did six months ago." I was in the best shape of my life, but was so dysmorphic I didn't know it. That night I was trying on clothes to decide what to bring to the West Coast. My skin was relatively calm and Julie's was breaking out.

"It's not fair," she said. "You have nothing on your skin right now. I hope you get a cold sore," she smirked from where she was sitting in my bed. And when I arrived in Portland, I did, and ended up shelling out money I didn't have on cold sore medicine at Whole Foods.

"How'd you get so beautiful?" my mom asked me one day, throwing me off kilter. She didn't often say stuff like that. We were at a bridal shower. My skin was somehow clear.

"No really," she continued after I rolled my eyes. "I'm nothing special, and neither is your dad. But you take care of yourself.

You take care of your skin and hair and you exercise." On the way home from the shower, I cried. *I have to stop. I am a fraud. I am scum of the earth. I am alone.*

One morning when I'd arrived home from a trip to the West Coast, I was texting with Julie. I was upset because though I loved these trips, they interrupted my exercise routine and I ate foods I normally wouldn't at home. I texted Julie something about thinking I gained weight on my trip. I told her I felt fat.

Your obsession with your body is getting really lame and gross, she shot back within seconds.

Unlike my face, I had a semblance of control around my body. I remember having lunch with my mother and telling her that watching people eat was disgusting to me, that I imagined the gross bowel movements they'd take. Did she do that? Was that normal? I asked her. No, she said. It was not.

Throughout all of this, I was still going to power yoga five days a week. Even after doing heroin. Once I was dry heaving into the toilet, but I shoved a piece of bread into my mouth and ran across the street to yoga. Yoga feels good. Opiates feel good. Together they felt like heaven. Sometimes, in between everything, I'd have revelatory days. Days when I'd had enough of my pathetic self-destruction. On those days, I read *When Things Fall Apart* by Pema Chödron and drank Smooth Move, trying to get all the toxins out of my body. I underlined sentences in the book that were meaningful to me. This was great for a few hours, and then I'd text my dealer, praying he wouldn't answer.

Heroin is exactly the opposite of being in the present moment but it tricks you into believing you are. I needed to spend money on some light-brown powder to put up my nose to feel like I was in the present moment. Feeling like I was in the present moment cost me a twenty-dollar bill. All I wanted was simple and yet the hardest thing to find: a sense of well-being. And I was using shortcuts. It fucking sucks to take the long way after knowing the shortcuts.

There's a memory that comes to me a couple of times a year. It's my friend Amanda in high school. We are either in class or in her car, her tiny white Geo Metro. That detail is lost, but I clearly remember her voice saying, "I don't get why you even do drugs. You're naturally happy. You're a naturally happy person."

I went from denying I had bad skin and avoiding the topic to acne being all I talked about. I couldn't have a conversation without bringing it up.

"What's wrong?" people asked.

My skin. My skin. My skin. I tried everything for my acne. I tried the hard stuff: benzoyl peroxide, Proactiv, and topicals like Differin and Duac gel. I tried antibiotics: doxycycline, minocycline, cephalexin, oracle. I tried tea: green, nettle, skin detox, healthy fasting, valerian root. I tried vitamins: milk thistle; Hair, Skin & Nails; zinc; fish oil. I tried restorative yoga, yin yoga, acupuncture, and lavender oil on my forehead. I tried meditating on having clear skin. I changed my pillowcases each night. I peed into containers and dipped a cotton ball into those containers and toned my face with my piss. I refused to take Accutane because the side effects freaked me out. At the end of my rope, I tried Ortho Tri-Cyclen, which turned me into a suicidal mess. I woke up thinking about guns and bullets. Ortho also gave me what dermatologists call "the initial breakout," which they claim is just your skin getting used to the new products, but the breakout was always so bad that it ended up being a worse hell than the original acne was. After having such terrible skin, you can live with anything. *Give me three cold sores and a huge pimple. Just not these cysts. Anything but these cysts*, you beg to the Acne Gods. When nothing worked, I just didn't leave my house. I was even embarrassed to meet my dealer. I kept my hair in front of my face and wore big, unflattering sunglasses. I wanted to look attractive so he would give me deals.

But then the heroin stopped working. The effects were muted, diminished. I told this to my friend, a recovering drug addict, and he said, "You could probably just eat dark chocolate at this point, and it would do the same thing." My tolerance was high. So was Julie's. We yelled at the dealer, telling him he was selling us shit. We sometimes joked he was actually selling us bareMinerals makeup, since it looked exactly like it. Maybe he was. We bought Suboxone and started to wean off. The only other option if we wanted the heroin to feel good again was to shoot it. And I wasn't going to do that. I was too skittish to even entertain the idea.

My yoga teacher at the time (who was straight edge, and in the metal band Youth of Today) loved telling our class that what feels like nectar in the beginning turns into poison in the long run, and what feels like poison in the beginning is nectar in the end. The greatest calamity, he liked to say, is not knowing when is enough. *Please shut up!* I would think, and leave the room for the bathroom. *I know. I know.* I heard you the first time.

The Music & the Boys

JANUARY. PARTYING LIKE it was 1999, because it was. It was the first New Year's Eve I took ecstasy. I was hooked! A boy at school put the small white pill with a smiley face on the front into my hand at the water fountain after Battle of the Bands. I had half-heartedly sung "Louie, Louie" and some Phish song with a friend's band. I was wearing the new teal turtleneck sweater my mother had given me for Christmas. Hours later, feeling the effects of ecstasy, a group of boys and I petted the sweater, deeming it *the softest sweater in the world.*

Getting ready to go to our separate events that night, my mother and I stood in the bathroom together putting on blush, and for the first time, she called me a bitch. Talking about this now she says, "You got *really* upset. I mean I thought of you as a bitch every day, it was just the first time I said it out loud!" and we laugh, but I remember the sting. A few days earlier my parents sat me down in the living room near the woodstove and told me they were separating.

◆ ◆ ◆

I guess I was a normal teenager. I was prone to silence and then to snotty remarks when I did talk. I was bratty and cranky and I and stayed out late and lied about where I was. I slept a shit ton. I had normal teen behavior that made parents worry. I stole lipstick and clothes. I drove home after a few Rolling Rocks. I kept baggies of weed and pipes in the back pockets of my skintight L.E.I. jeans and sometimes would hide beers in my room. But I didn't have an eating disorder, I didn't cut, I wasn't clinically depressed, so I was, overall, "fine."

When my parents decided on this temporary separation, I was fourteen. I painted the walls around my bed black. I wore a black hoodie.

"Black because that's how you feel on the inside?" my dad teased me.

My mom tells me now I handled the separation "too well." She says I comforted her, because she was so upset: feeling guilty, thinking she was a bad person, a bad mom. I didn't want her to feel these emotions. I was relieved my parents separated. I'd always picked up on their tension and hated their fights during car rides, and I was freed from that now. I didn't grieve their separation myself—that would draw attention to it. I just pretended it wasn't going on.

◆ ◆ ◆

Using that CoverGirl blush in the bathroom with my mother ("You're pale, put some color on your cheeks," she'd say), she told me the compact was broken, the plastic lid was falling off.

"It's not broken," I said.

"It's broken!" she said. "God, sometimes it's like you're in denial."

In the book *The Fantasy Bond*, Robert Firestone explains that children need to believe their parents are good, that everything is well and loving, because if they see the truth, they will crumble in the face of reality. It's odd my mother would say something that profound because of a CoverGirl blush. Even now, it embarrasses me to think about—that she nailed me so hard.

◆ ◆ ◆

I loved tanning. Waking and baking. Gwen Stefani. I secretly loved Tori Amos and wrote her lyrics on my bedroom wall in Sharpie. During the school day, I hit my bowl in the bathroom and blew the smoke into the toilet. I'd receive my math tests back; I didn't care about the thirties and forties I'd get on them. I'd just throw them in the garbage. Failing school did not bother me. I had many friends and that's what really mattered in high school. My academic performance (or lack thereof) might have had something to do with the separation, but it could still be excused as normal teenager stuff, so no one really called me out. Once in a while my parents sat me down at the table with pamphlets for dance and art classes. We'd have these little meetings together even though they were separated.

"We want you to do more extracurricular stuff," my mom said. "This collage class looks really cool."

"Then *you* take it!" I said. My dad laughed.

My mom did end up enrolling a friend and me in the collage class. No one else showed up, and my mom wrote a letter to the program, demanding her money back. The whole point, she said, was for me to socialize with new people.

◆ ◆ ◆

My circle of friends consisted of two other girls and three boys. We girls referred to the boys as *the boys*. "What time are the boys getting here?" "Should we invite the boys?" "Did the boys call while I was in the shower?" We'd go to Crossgates Mall, and the boys asked for free Orange Julius samples while the girls went to Supercuts to get bangs. We saw *You've Got Mail* and *Titanic*. Sometimes we sat in a circle and played our own version of spin the bottle. When the bottle landed on you, you had to flash a body part. The girls would flash their pubic hair or breasts, and the boys, their penises. "I'd show them my butt before I'd show them my *vagina*," Mary said.

I was closest to Nat, and from when we were twelve until the end of high school, I'd sleep at his house some weekends, *Dawson's Creek*–style but better, because no one was secretly in love with the other. We spoke on the phone for hours and had contests over who could make their throat cackle longer. We had a secret, the "call back at midnight." Our parents made us hang up at nine p.m., but we'd sneak our cordless phones back into bed and call each other again at midnight, to chat more. Because of "call back at midnight," our song was "Runaway Train" by Soul Asylum. *Call you up in the middle of the night, like a firefly without a light, you were there like a blowtorch burning, I was a key that could use a little turning.* When "Runaway Train" comes on the radio, I still crank it and crack the windows.

I got my own phone, one of those clear ones you could see the colored wires through. I thought it was cool as shit. At Nat's bar mitzvah, we sang Smash Mouth and Sugar Ray with the karaoke machine. He taught me swing dance moves and spins, and we did "the fish," where one of us mimed reeling in a fish with a line, and the other swam in. We had a code in the classroom: when one of us clicked our tongue, it meant, *Look at me, I have something to tell you. I just observed something funny. Click, click.*

. . .

We pointed out and knew each other's quirks. When I'd ask Nat for a sip of his drink, he'd say, "I hate the way your spit gets cold on the bottle by the time you hand it back to me. I hate *cold spit.*" Eating at our local pizzeria he said, "Whenever you open your mouth to take a bite of pizza, you open it really wide but take a small bite. Let me show you what it looks like." I knew he slept with either his butt or arm straight up in the air. I saw him like that when I'd get up to pee.

Sometimes I'd tell Nat at unexpected times I wanted to stop being friends. It was dramatic—I'd choose a time we were getting along swimmingly to catch him off guard. He wouldn't understand, of course, and would get upset, to the point of crying.

"I have to go," I remember him saying through tears.

Maybe this behavior helped me feel like I'd regained control of what I'd lost. Or maybe I was reenacting what was going on in my own home. Maybe I thought blowups and blowouts and harsh words were what love was supposed to look like. I carried that with me through most of my twenties. When I was twenty-two and in love for the first time, I woke up and said to my boyfriend Simon:

"We were so *nice* to each other last night!"

"Why do you always say that?" he replied, genuinely perplexed. "Don't you get that's how we're supposed to be?"

• • •

Nat's house was deep in the woods, and he never let you forget that Wyley Gates murdered his father, father's girlfriend, brother, and orphaned toddler cousin just down the road in 1986, the year we were both born. But Nat's efforts to freak me out didn't work, because I found his home cozy. Frank Sinatra sang in the background, and there was always a ping-pong game to play or a hot tub to get into. Nat's bedroom had two twin beds and its own bathroom attached. We'd gossip in our separate beds, competitively seeing who could eat more clementines. I have no recollection of his parents fighting, only of waking up to music and breakfast and conversations over the crossword puzzle.

One of my earliest memories is sitting with my mother in the kitchen, my dad on the couch a few feet away. We were eating frozen mini Snickers, and my mom threw one at my dad to catch and eat, but it smacked him hard on his bald head.

At Nat's house they got their couches redone, green, I wrote in my journal.

• • •

Nat was persuasive and perceptive in a way that entertained me. He studied people's behavior, often picking up on someone's tiny mannerism and imitating it back to them before maniacally laughing. He had a strong streak of schadenfreude: he persuaded me to jump off of his roof onto his trampoline, to eat a cat food sandwich, to watch the psychological thriller *Misery* before bed. I played along. He fed me many lines—some true and some false—that stuck with me for years, like girls can hold it if they have to pee but boys can't, and a normal reaction to someone dying is laughing, because of the shock. He told me the lead singer from Blues Traveler died from being so obese that he exploded.

Nat was passionate about pranks and loved the novelty store Spencer's. He kept fart spray on his bedside table, once spraying me so much I had to leave a party to take a shower. Taking a walk through a stream one summer, he staged a fall to look like he'd cracked his head open. I believed him until his fake crying turned into laughter—he'd brought blood capsules with him. One time—only once and he never did it or spoke of it again—Nat showed up at my house dressed in a suit and hat and mustache. He stayed in character all night while my mom drove us to various places—the pizza joint, the bank—and Nat's character (a Mafia don) pretended this was all new to him. He had a Jersey accent, and his name was Sal.

We were an odd pair. I'd grown faster; I was taller and had big boobs. Nat was petite. We both bit our nails to the quick. They were ugly and near bleeding. We loved to compare whose were worse. He always thought mine were more disgusting, and I thought his were more disgusting. Really, they were the same. When Nat went to Miami or soccer camp in France, he'd send me postcards and address them to "sis." I called him "bro." We took our birthdays seriously. Nat gave me bracelets and Macy Gray and Enya CDs, and I gave him hemp necklaces, hats, and once a T-shirt that read *No really. What's wrong with your face?*

. . .

Nat's parents drove us to New York City, and on the way in they'd do trivia with us, which bridge was which. I'd go to the Strand and look at books with his mother, and Nat, bored by books, tried on jeans next door at Mavi, admiring himself in the mirror. Nat was familiar with New York City and more in the know with what was cool than I was. He'd tell me about the new sippable chocolate we had to try at Starbucks. When his parents let us have a few hours alone, we went to Ben & Jerry's for milkshakes and walked around Saint Mark's, taking photos of each other with a disposable camera next to blow-up penises and wearing Bob Marley dreadlock wigs. We agreed we'd both live in New York City when we grew up. We were both pigeon-toed and dragged our feet while we walked.

"Pick up your feet, you guys," Nat's mom would say.

Our friendship made me feel special. Many of our friends' parents were scandalized when they learned Nat and I had sleepovers. Nat's parents and my mom seemed to think it was pretty banal, but you could tell they actually thought it was rare and special. My dad never knew anything about it, I don't think.

◆ ◆ ◆

On Monday nights I had dinner at my dad's apartment. As I got older, he'd allow me half a glass of wine while we ate. He was never much of a cook, and the dinners he made were bizarre. The scene at my dad's was not far off from *The Squid and the Whale*, Noah Baumbach's film about a divorce. The boys go to their father's new apartment for dinner every other week. The father shows his son what will be his new desk, and the son looks at it and says, "But Dad? This is a left-handed desk." The father drops the meatloaf on the floor and serves it anyway.

One of the rare occasions my brother, Trevor, was home, he peeked in the fridge, pulled out a tub of mozzarella balls, looked at me, and said, "Who does Dad think he is?" I didn't hear about *The Squid and the Whale* until my midtwenties, and when I finally watched it I related deeply. My mom had recommended it, but won't watch it with me because she says it hits too close to home.

My mom started hanging out with another divorced woman, Carol, who wore a dozen silver bangles on her wrists and had a raspy voice and peppy personality. "Chloe, always remember to exercise," she told me once. Carol was fit and tan and loved the

Chili Peppers, so the boys and I respected her. They'd drive us to shows: Marcy Playground, Weezer, Joan Jett, Dave Matthews Band, Eve 6, Goo-Goo Dolls, and Fuel. In the car, the boys impersonated the *Dumb and Dumber* call and response:

"Mock."

"Yeah!"

"Ing."

"Yeah!"

"Bird."

"Yeah!"

"Yeah."

"Yeah!"

The only word the boys yelled more than that song was "Shotgun!" And then there was the song "New Age Girl" by Deadeye Dick.

"She don't eat meat but she sure likes the bone!"

◆ ◆ ◆

Three months after the separation, I went to one therapy appointment. My mom was going to therapy at the time, and she'd also packed a backpack and left for a weeklong silent meditation retreat at Omega Institute. She lived in a tent for three nights. She claims this trip and the Pema Chödrön books she was reading "saved her life." My appointment was on a Sunday at three p.m. and my mom had plans, so my dad had to take me. The boys had slept over the night before and were still sleeping when my dad arrived. They rolled out of bed and piled into the car with me. I wore a tight fuchsia v-neck T-shirt and regretted it, feeling busty and embarrassed for dressing that way in front of my dad and the boys.

I panicked and cried hard through the session. I said I thought my mom had had an affair. When I came out of the office, the boys were in the waiting room silently flipping through *Sassy* and *YM* magazines. My dad had gone grocery shopping. We stood outside the building and waited for him to pull up, climbed back into the car, clicked on the radio. I didn't go to therapy again for ten years.

. . .

"Can't your kid go anywhere without a friend?" my uncle asked my mom at a family party.

The sleepover lifestyle was both comforting and distracting. There were so many alternating dynamics between my mom, my dad, my brother, and me. 4×3×2×1, mathematically. You never knew which two would be bonding and which two would be in a nasty argument. It could get tense and depressing quickly. My family was on better behavior if a friend was there. When my friends' moms came to pick them up in the mornings, dread and loneliness crept over me and stayed for the rest of the day, until I slept it off.

. . .

The tension slowly dissipated from my house. There were no frozen Snickers bars flying into people's heads anymore. My dad lived fifteen minutes away. Trevor was accepted at Simon's Rock, an early college for gifted high schoolers in Great Barrington, Massachusetts, and he lived there now. When he *was* home, he and my mom lay on the couch in the dark with candles lit, yelling along with Bob Dylan and Patti Smith. They'd ask me to watch movies or lie in the dark with them, but I wouldn't hear of it. I hated movies. I read in my mom's journal she felt like we'd gone overnight from a family of four to a family of two. One night we had to figure out how to jump-start her car on our own, both terrified we'd get electrocuted. When we did it correctly, we jumped up and down, saying, "Hallelujah!" One summer evening, we bought a pizza and a bottle of wine to drink on the porch. My mom couldn't work the corkscrew, and a process that should have taken two minutes turned into half an hour, ending with a corked bottle of wine and both of us in frustrated tears. When my mom got a CD player installed in her Saturn, we screamed with joy. We entered 10,000 Maniacs into the slot, and thought the word that appeared said *Lord*. We thought it was so weird, and no one was there to tell us we were wrong, that it in fact read *Load*.

. . .

The boys showed up uninvited, requesting Newman's lemonade and popsicles. We had one of those small basketball hoops attached to a beam going through my living room and a blue Nerf basketball. The boys' basketball games become so rowdy and went on for so long that I hated when they played basketball. I was left out.

"We need a backboard!" they'd complain. They came up with the idea to nail one of my *Seventeen* magazines to the beam. My mom was annoyed at the volume and chaos of the games too, so we started hiding the Nerf ball in the freezer before the boys came over. On those nights they were disappointed and would look around at length for the ball while my mom and I pretended we had no idea where it could be. My mom and I got questions about the *Seventeen* magazine backboard for years to come. Sarah Michelle Gellar was on the cover.

The boys sprawled on the living room floor and went through the records my dad hadn't taken yet: the Kinks, Cream, the Doors. We had Guess Who? and Scattergories marathons and made cookies-and-cream milkshakes while big black ants scampered around the blue counter. We repeatedly watched the *Behind the Music* episode of Blind Melon. They listened earnestly while I read personal essays aloud from *Chicken Soup for the Teenage Soul*. They tried on my dresses and bras and heels. We slept head to toe in my twin bed with my pink comforter. At night we propped our chins on our hands and talked about what we hoped for after high school. The boys said they wanted to see if they could make something of their band in California.

I remember what their plans were, but I don't remember my own plans, or if I even had any.

.   .   .

We had to leave buckets around the house to catch the water from the leaks in the roof, and my mom would scream when she'd find a dead mouse in the dryer. I'd stay calm in the wake of her panic and put a baggie around my hand, retrieve it, and chuck it outside. During power outages from thunderstorms, we lit candles and feared we'd get electrocuted if we touched the refrigerator. (Years later at my dad's, he asked why I was reading instead of working on my computer, and I told him I was afraid of being electrocuted. "You lived with your mother too long," he said.)

Raccoons sometimes gnawed through our screen door into the house, and I listened to mice scurry through my bedroom walls while I fell asleep. "I smell rotten eggs!" one of the boys said, referring to our sulfur water, something that embarrassed me for years. "Chloe smells like a woodstove," my friends said, not negatively but not positively either. On days I was at my dad's, my mom told me she went to the library after work as to not come home to a cold and empty house. My mom's financial state wasn't awesome, and she took a second job waitressing on the weekends. She'd borrow money from my brother's savings, and left little IOU, ♥ *Mom* notes around the house.

It wasn't only my spirits the boys lifted; it was my mother's too. She never sent anyone away, always opened our screen door warmly. My mom was taking a photography class at a community college, so she often used the boys and me as her subjects; she took photos of us sitting on the counter, eating blue freeze pops, reading *Rolling Stone*. The boys loved making grilled sandwiches with salami and cheese and balsamic vinegar for us. We tried to make the sandwiches on our own, but they never tasted as good when we did it. My mom was big on keeping daily gratitude journals and sentence-a-day journals at that point, and I'd read them.

Drove Chloe and the boys to pizza and a movie.

Chloe and the boys kept me up all night, too loud.

Chloe laid on me tonight while we watched Gilmore Girls.

Chloe reminded me tonight to stop complaining about driving them everywhere, because soon I won't be anymore. So true!

Nat and Chloe are in New York City, I hope they're making good memories.

Chloe has eight kids here. They obviously think this is the party house, but sometimes they take it too far.

My relationship with my mom was decent at the base level, but we'd have blowouts, yelling and slamming doors, retreating to our rooms. I was embarrassed at how when she shifted gears, her long armpit hair showed. One of the boys joked, "I like your mom's hippie armpit hair." She was embarrassed (and concerned) about my party-girl behavior and hated the photos of me with a cigarette in one hand, giving the middle finger with the other. "I'd rather have you smoke pot than cigarettes," she'd say.

I liked the artificial things my mother avoided: spray-on deodorant, mascara, L'Oréal blond hair dye, neon colors, cigarettes. I resented her lavender lotion and earth-tones-only policy. She told me not to dye my hair so blond, not to go tanning so frequently, that being pale was a sign of health, not to shave above the knee. Now I wish I'd listened. And I love lavender lotion.

Nat was good for my depression. One night lounging on couches at his house, he suggested a walk, even though it was below freezing outside, pitch black, a few feet of snow on the ground.

"A walk?" I asked incredulously.

"Yeah. People take *walks*, believe it or not. It's a real thing real people do."

+ + +

The landline rang and rang, and the cordless phone was often lost or dead because I hadn't charged it. Nat would call, saying, "Listen to this," and play Lauryn Hill or Shaggy or Nelly Furtado's new song into the phone. "Can you come over and braid my hair?" he'd ask, some summers rocking a head of tiny braids. My mom drove us to movies. She went to see *Chocolat*, and the boys and I went to *Save the Last Dance*, where the boys decided Julia Stiles is an "ugly crier." It was winter, and I hadn't shaved my legs for months.

"Wanna feel something gross?" I asked Nat, sticking my leg out. He acted horrified and talked about it for the next few years.

.   .   .

For tenth grade, Mary and Sarah were sent to private schools, while the boys and I stayed in public school in Chatham. The boys and I invented a game we played in the car. I'd be in the front, since it was usually my mom or dad driving. I'd hit the "seek" button, and the game was to call out the band or artist in that second before the song changed. I was failing school with a vengeance, but I fucking killed at this game.

"Robyn!"

"Coldplay!"

"Michelle Branch!"

"Shakira!"

"Savage Garden!"

"Eric Clapton!"

I was desperate to win. In school, the boys took advanced placement classes while I continued to struggle. I was supposed to see tutors and attend after-school help sessions and summer school, but I failed and skipped those activities too. When the boys talked about biology or history or sports, I couldn't add anything. One afternoon after an English-class discussion about *Animal Farm*, the bell rang and Nat and I walked to our lockers.

"It's really funny how you do that," Nat said, kneeling in front of his messy locker.

"Do what?"

"Like, I can tell you haven't read the book, but you participate in the conversation anyway, and, like, say general observations anyone could say having not read the book. It's hilarious." He began laughing just thinking about it, throwing his head back, brown eyes sparkling, mouth wide.

He was absolutely right. I hadn't known it was so obvious.

I got really into No Doubt's first two albums, *No Doubt* and *The Beacon Street Collection*. Since I knew the boys weren't familiar with them, I concocted a lie to impress them. I chose one of the songs and wrote my own lyrics to it and told the boys I'd written a song. I sang it to them. They told me it was pretty cool. I did the same thing to my dad with a Jewel song called "Near You Always." My dad was really proud of me and had me record it on a tape for him.

．　．　．

I took long naps after school when I was coming down from doing bong rips. My mom blasted Lucinda Williams to wake me up for dinner. Years later, she told me "Lonely Girls" was her theme song. She laughed after she said it. The song goes *Lonely girls, lonely girls, heavy blankets, heavy blankets, heavy blankets cover lonely girls.* This was the first time I realized my mother had been depressed. "Go to yoga!" Trevor and I sometimes encouraged her, knowing she'd come back in a better mood than she'd left in.

My mom and I ate salad with grilled chicken on the couch and watched *Gilmore Girls* and *Will & Grace*. My dad and I watched *That '70s Show* and ate Freihofer's cookies by the handful. My dad tried to make me feel at home. He wanted to buy me duplicates of the stuff I had at my mom's, but I resisted. Two of everything seemed excessive and depressing. "I don't need two boom boxes," I'd say. "I have one at Mom's."

My parents both stopped buying Christmas trees. Why should they? It was just me, and I was a teenager who did not care about decorating trees or rituals. I'd complained, when the four of us still lived in the house, about walking down the hall in a line with candles and singing "Silent Night" and was happy to be free from it. Some years my mom brought home a plant and called it a Charlie

Brown Christmas tree, and my dad put a plastic decorative white cone on the dinner table. My mom still made holidays special for me though; she liked causally celebrating Epiphany, and she'd give me three small gifts for each of the three kings a few weeks after Christmas.

Since we were each going through our separate mournings, I had fewer eyes on me and more times of the day when no one knew where I was or what I was doing. At my dad's, I had junk food like Cheez-Its and butter crunch ice cream. I could sneak out when I heard him snoring at night and walk the train tracks to the boys' houses. I'd put twenty dollars in a makeup compact and throw it out my window, where my friend would catch it, fill it with weed, and throw it back.

No one ever made me do my homework. Or they pretended to believe me when I said I'd already done it. At this rate, I wouldn't get into college, not that I wanted to go. My journal switches from innocently speaking of a drama club play I was in to sounding like *Go Ask Alice*.

Mostly I just drink and smoke.

I loved smoking weed out of a seltzer can or an apple and watching the reality shows *elimiDATE* and *Bzzz!* after my mom had gone to bed, blowing the smoke out my window.

. . .

Maybe I didn't think I had a right to admit I was sad. My life had mostly been easy. Lots of kids' parents were split up. Though my parents were separating, they loved me. I had a roof over my head. I wrote regularly, filling up a few journals a year, but I never wrote about my parents. I wrote about drugs and parties and my deep love for my friends and made exhaustive lists (*Boys Houses I've Slept At* and *People I've Hung Out with Sober and Unsober*). My real brother was gone, but the boys were my brothers. I had no real boyfriend, but they were my boyfriends. They could see what was going on and were there for me, literally—occupying space with me, sleeping head to toe with me in my twin bed, offering emotional solace that can still tug my heart now, when I think too much about it.

◆　◆　◆

When we turned sixteen, the boys and I took drivers' ed together. Our teacher was in his seventies and often fell asleep in the passenger seat. The boys and I laughed in the back while Nat hit every pothole he could on purpose. Sometimes we persuaded our teacher to let us drive to Dairy Queen for blizzards. That summer we were into Jimi Hendrix, Rancid, Bush, Nirvana, and Stone Temple Pilots.

My dad taught me to drive stick on his red Jetta. When I got my permit, he came to pick me up for school and turned the car to face down the driveway. I'd only driven in grocery store parking lots, and he was letting me drive to school. This upset my mom. Driving with my parents was two different experiences: my dad let me listen to music but my mom bit the insides of her cheeks and gave exasperated sighs of anxiety. I turned the volume up; she turned it down. I turned it back up. She turned it back down.

Despite our lazy drivers' ed, we got our licenses right away, Nat first, then me. My mom passed me down her green stick-shift Saturn, and Nat had a black Jeep. Nat loved finding little stands out in the country where we could get cheeseburgers and ice cream cones. We liked to go cruising and were obsessed with the *American Pie* 1 and 2 soundtracks—we both knew every word to every song. I'm ashamed to admit his favorites were by Sum 41 and Tonic, and mine was "Sway" by Bic Runga. The first time I drove anywhere on my own, it was to Coconuts, where I bought CAKE and Sublime CDs. Then I drove to Dunkin' Donuts for a bagel.

Driving let us find out what we wanted to do when our parents weren't around. We could eat as many ninety-nine-cent McChickens (extra mayo!) and drink as many gas station hot chocolates as we wanted, and I could buy the smelly vanilla car fresheners I loved and my mom hated, and hang crosses (because they were trendy) from my rearview mirror. We could take road trips to Northampton and the mall—the *big* mall, the *cool* mall, not the small hippie mall in bum-fuck Massachusetts where my mom would take us because malls gave her headaches. I didn't have to listen to my mom sing along with *Bye, bye, Miss American Pie* or Bob Marley anymore.

We'd smoke weed in beautiful swimming holes or pavilions or secret spots. We were always thirsty, and Nat spent his allowance on trendy drinks. Mine went to weed that I kept in Altoid containers. He loved Vitaminwater, coconut water, and Gatorade. When Nat hit a bunny, he pulled over and we both cried. When I threw my Snapple bottle out the window, he backed up the Jeep and made me get it. One time I was trying to quit smoking weed, and we went to a waterfall—I threw all my pipes and papers into the water. Nat took photos of me with a disposable camera to document the day.

I loved driving: along dirt roads, back roads, all roads, with my tapes and CDs, weed, and cigarettes. Driving was such intoxicating freedom, and the smell of manure that permeated my favorite back roads had an almost orgasmic scent to me. My parents weren't communicating so much with each other, so I could ask my mom if I could drive my car with some friends to Montreal, and when she said no, ask my dad, who said yes. I went with my dad's answer.

Around the same time we began buying beer with fake IDs, we listened to the Canadian band Spirit of the West. We played caps and beer pong, which I thought was called Beirut, because the boys called it that. We played Kings and Assholes. We dipped our fingers in our beers to make the foam go down. I stuck my chewing gum on top of my can of Budweiser. I brought white chocolate Flipz to parties along with a case of Coors Light or Rolling Rock or Bud. I was "the cool girl." The boys didn't look at me sexually, and I liked that. It made me feel safe and accepted. "Bring girls," the boys told me before every party. "Bring some girls." I was so cool I wasn't even a girl anymore.

◆   ◆   ◆

We had an old shed to next to our house my dad used to do carpentry in. My friends and I cleaned it out and made a sign calling it the Clubhouse. I had huge parties; we'd play darts and drink beer and smoke Marlboro Reds. My mom took everyone's keys, and they'd all sleep over. The boys at this point had known her for years and called her Shelly (no one else had ever called her this in her life), and when they were drunk enough, they'd go up the stairs to her bedroom, begging her to come hang out with us.

"Please, Shelly."

*   *   *

The day the new Red Hot Chili Peppers album *By the Way* came out, Nat and I drove forty-five minutes to Coconuts to buy it. We took the excursion seriously. "Shhh," Nat said to me each time I tried to talk during it. "Stop talking. I'm trying to hear the lyrics." After a few listens we both knew every word, singing together in unison, thrusting our bare arms out our windows to feel the wind and sun.

Senior year of high school we were still close, but the dynamics had changed. People were having sex. Each weekend we danced for hours in a huge barn that had a mirrored wall. We danced and sang as loud as we could to Kanye, Jack Johnson, and Destiny's Child. We sang Britney Spears's "Toxic" and OutKast's "Hey Ya!" and all the hits by Nelly. We woke up with our throats scratched raw. The toilet would be clogged with someone's vomit, and my hair would smell like smoke, from cigarettes and bonfires.

In our high school yearbook, parents were to secretly write something to their child and submit it along with a baby photo. My mom had written, *Sundown yellow moon, I replay the past, I know every scene by heart, they all went by too fast.* I was both mortified and thrilled my mom left a Bob Dylan quote in my yearbook. No one else's mom did that. At graduation, she took photographs of me and the boys as we walked to get our diplomas. She got them developed in black and white. Each of us, in our separate photos, are looking directly into her camera, our black hats on our heads. When I asked her how she got those shots, she said, "I yelled their names when they walked by, so they'd look up at me before I snapped."

◆ ◆ ◆

I moved to Brooklyn—taking Nat's brown Banana Republic sweater with me—and when Nat graduated from Oberlin, he did too. We met up at Beauty Bar shortly after he arrived. On the phone I'd warned him I'd gotten fat. When I arrived at the bar he said, "You didn't get fat—oh man! I'd actually *really* been looking forward to that!"

Nat slept over that night, and in the morning I left him snoring in a fetal position on my futon with a carton of poutine one centimeter from his face.

◆ ◆ ◆

Throughout my twenties I looked for other guys and groups of guys to be my best friends, to take me in, to make me one of them, to feel that sense of camaraderie again, but I always felt paranoid they thought I was hitting on them. Eventually I gave up, accepting the fact I would never have a group of guy friends again. I pretended to be o.k. with it, but I felt slightly jealous, a familiar dull ache in my chest, when I saw other girls who did.

My parents stayed separated for fifteen years and then finalized their divorce. My mom starting seeing someone, and at the same time, I brought my boyfriend Simon home for the first time from New York City. Both guys slept over. "I figure we're both adults now," my mom said earnestly. "*Both* of us!" I said, and we giggled.

My mother remarried in May of 2014, and Nat married the following summer. Nat and I hadn't seen each other for a few years before his wedding.

"We used to be *inseparable*," we told a group of people at the reception at one point, linking arms. I started getting emotional.

"Oh, boy," he said, laughing at me, "here we go."

"Sorry," I said, wiping my eyes, careful of my mascara.

"Are you kidding?" he answered. "I love this stuff! I live for it."

During Beyoncé's "Love on Top," I grabbed the hand of Nat's gorgeous bride and spun her into the only dance moves I know.

"Oh my *God*," she yelled over the music, "you dance *exactly* like Nat."

"Oh, yeah," I yelled back. "He taught me how."

Failing Singing

WHEN MY CHILDHOOD FRIEND Amanda meets one of my new friends or someone I'm dating, she loves to play the singing card. She tells them I used to sing. She asks me to sing. She tells them I used to sing *Beauty and the Beast* in the car. I want to kill her when she does this. I feel guilt-tripped and defensive.

At a shitty bar in the East Village a few months ago, Amanda started in on me.

"She used to sing! Come on, do it. Do it."

My arms crossed over my chest.

"Can we change the subject now?" I asked.

"You don't understand," she defended herself. "When you're just 'O.K.' at everything, and your friends around you are superstars, it's hard."

"Dude, I was a normal person who could sing a little," I said. "Anyway, who wants to hear about the worst lie Amanda and I ever told?"

Hungover and over each other in the car driving back upstate the next day, I said, "You really like to tell people about my singing when you're drunk."

"I know," Amanda said.

"It's very annoying for me."

I did find it annoying and embarrassing, enraging even. But I also appreciated that she was showing other layers of me to the people I was sleeping with, because it made me seem more interesting and complex. More talented.

"Sorry," Amanda said, not because she wanted to say it but because she knew I wanted to hear it. She rolled down her window. Lit a Marlboro Light. I reached for the volume knob and turned up Taylor Swift and didn't sing along. We changed the subject and discussed how we can't believe we'll be thirty in six months. "I thought there would be more," Amanda said, kidding but not.

◆ ◆ ◆

When I tell people I used to sing, their eyebrows go up in a way I despise. They look at me differently, as though they want me to sing for them on the spot. As though I'm suddenly worthy of their attention. This is when the shutdown begins in my body. I *used* to sing, I say. Downplay. Past tense. Arms over chest. Avert the eyes. Head down.

The excuses I give when I tell people I do not sing anymore:

(1) I'm in the business of writing, and I got a yoga teacher training certificate. Do I really need to add one more "career" to my list of careers that make no money? (People kind of see my point when I say that, or pretend to.)

(2) I lost my muscle for it. It's a muscle—like all skills—and when you don't do it, it weakens and eventually goes away. (The reaction to this one is most annoying, because people want to tell you you're wrong, like when you tell someone you've put on weight, and they tell you that you didn't, but you know you are right.)

(3) It's too expensive. When I moved to New York City, I couldn't afford it (and didn't care enough to ask my parents to help me out).

An elderly man in my memoir class found out I "used to" sing one night on our walk to the train. He was telling me about the voice lessons he was taking down the street. I told him I used to sing and that I stopped, I don't anymore.

"That's not good," he responded, shaking his head.

Telling people you stopped singing is something you regret the moment the words leave your mouth. It's meant to impress, but it backfires and disappoints. It just makes you look like a loser. A giver-upper. A has-been. Possibly even a liar. Because you might have an inflated opinion of your singing, of yourself. How do people know you were actually good at it, especially since they will never hear you sing? It's like telling someone you're an incredible cook but you don't cook anymore—will never cook again—and have nothing to show of your cooking. And getting mad when people talk about your cooking.

"Singing changes your brain," *TIME* magazine says. "When you sing, musical vibrations move through you, altering your physical and emotional landscape." The articles about how good singing is for you almost hurt my feelings, as though they are written to make me personally feel bad.

◆ ◆ ◆

The first music I fell in love with as a child was the girl groups of the fifties and sixties. I liked the Marvelettes, the Ronettes, and the Chordettes, anything that ended with "ettes," really. I was into Dusty Springfield and Lesley Gore and Frankie Lymon. Hearing the songs "Johnny Angel," "Please Mr. Postman," and "Goody Goody" made me feel the way Mary Karr says her first drink made her feel: a sunflower bloomed in my chest. I still feel that way when I hear these songs. I have the record in my apartment now *Girl Groups, Golden Archive Series*. Three dollars. I like to play it on Christmas Eve.

People realized I could sing when I was in second grade. My class was doing a play called *The Tooth Fairy*. The teacher gave me the solo, which I still know by heart. I had to step out of the group to the front of the stage and sing, *We can't eat apples or corn on the cob, and saying our S's is sometimes a job, it's worth it as long as the fairies will pay; it won't bother us when the grown-ups say* . . . Then I stepped back into the rest of the group and we sang together, mocking the grown-ups.

I felt special and singled out; I simultaneously liked that feeling and was embarrassed by it. My parents used to have a recording of the performance on VHS, and I notice when I take that step back into the group, I look behind me before I step, worried I'll trip or bump into someone. My body language is "Look at me! No, actually don't."

After that second-grade breakout performance, each summer I was in plays put on by a company in Spencertown called Stageworks. In fifth grade, I joined the school drama club. I started taking voice lessons and I went on auditions and I performed in plays with various local theater companies. At my auditions, I sang the Carole King song "Chicken Soup with Rice." The song is almost five minutes long—it goes through each of the twelve months—so the team of directors usually cut me off halfway through. They would say, "We already know you can sing."

One of the companies went to New York City to do a fifteen-minute showcase. We sang "Seasons of Love" from the *Rent* soundtrack. *I'm 14 and yet I performed in New York City!!!!!!!!!* I wrote in my journal.

I loved the nerve-wracking adrenaline buildup, suspense, and crash of going on auditions. I still love this trajectory and have re-created it with readings and public-speaking events and with lovers. I liked having my hair French braided and foundation caked onto my face by the stage moms (my mom was not one of them). The auditions didn't intimidate me because whether I was good or not wasn't up for interpretation. It wasn't subjective. I was clearly good. In middle school, you either could sing or you couldn't, and *solo* was the word of envy among adolescent girls. Or maybe that was just me.

◆ ◆ ◆

There was a CD I had called *The Broadway Kids*. This was my ultimate goal: to be a Broadway kid. To be in the photo on the cover wearing jeans and a T-shirt.

My parents and I went to dozens of musicals. What annoys people about musicals is precisely what I like about them: the optimism, the breaking into song out of nowhere, the over-enunciation, the dramatizing of feelings. I pored over the headshots and the bios of the actors, imagining what mine would say one day. During the scenes of choreographed synchronized dancing, I'd choose one girl in the crowd and appoint her future-me. That would be me when I grew up and was a successful actor/singer/dancer. My whole family would watch me and be proud. I would be a backup dancer with the chorus, but I would also get all of the main roles—I'd be Liesl in *The Sound of Music*, Kim in *Bye Bye Birdie*, Maria in *West Side Story*, Kathy Selden in *Singin' in the Rain*, Sheila Bryant in *A Chorus Line*, Sandy in *Grease*, and Dorothy in *The Wizard of Oz*. I owned cassette tapes of all of these plays and spent hours upon hours belting in my living room when I was home alone. When I sang along to oldies on the radio—I could never commit to which part I wanted to sing, backup or lead vocals, so I'd sing both, cutting myself off, making whomever I was with laugh.

My singing was strongest, and my acting and dancing tied for last behind it. Belting was meant as a compliment back then. "She can *belt*," classmates would say about the good singers in school. I'd spend the next few years with vocal teachers who had to redo all of my belting and teach me how to use my voice properly. But, I knew, the better you belted, the more parts you got.

I became educated about adult matters through cassettes and musical theater. I learned the word *résumé* and *affair* and *divorce* and *hussy*. I learned about masochism and sex and poverty. I learned about childhood trauma and ambition and body dysmorphia (*A Chorus Line*) and hormones and puberty (*Bye Bye Birdie*) and death and racism (*West Side Story*) and mean dads and good nannies (*Sound of Music*).

I was in *CATS*. *You're a Good Man, Charlie Brown*. *Alice in Concert*. *Anything Goes*. *A Midsummer Night's Dream*. In *Once Upon a Mattress*, I played Lady Larkin, the same role Sarah Jessica Parker played on Broadway. But I didn't get the lead roles—I got the second lead in every play I did. There was a girl one year older than me, Heather Rowe, who beat me out for all the leads. The only time I got the lead was in *You're a Good Man, Charlie Brown*, and the only reason I got it was because Heather was playing Annie for a *real* theater company and had to sit drama club out. I went to see her star in *Annie*, pure jealousy pumping through my veins.

I learned and accepted early on that there will always be someone more successful than you at what you're doing. I didn't even know if I wanted the big roles Heather got—didn't know if I was up for the responsibility and commitment. If she ever got sick, I knew all her lines and notes by heart. But of course she never got sick.

Heather invited me to her house for dinner once. I remember feeling uncomfortable. I remember her having a horse, but I might be making that up. I reciprocated and invited her to my house for dinner a few weeks later. In the bathroom when we were washing our hands before we ate, I turned on both faucets and said, "I never know which one the warm one is."

"Isn't it usually the left one?" she said.

*   *   *

From ages ten to twenty, I went through five different vocal teachers. I was most consistent with Mary—Wednesdays after school at four p.m. for three years. Mary ate toast and jam, slurping and crunching loudly, while I rehearsed. She yelled at me if I'd eaten ice cream with my friends beforehand. This was a normal kid thing we'd do, and this was sort of an insight that made me wonder, how can I do both? Be a professional singer and also a normal teenager? Singing seemed to want a lot from me.

At most auditions I'd have to perform both a song and a monologue, so Mary would assign me songs with monologues preceding them. My favorite was *The Fantasticks* monologue that leads up to the song "Much More."

I am sixteen years old and every day something different happens to me. I hug myself till my arms turn blue, and then I close my eyes and I cry and cry till the tears come down and I can taste them—I love to taste my tears—I am special, I am special. Please, God, please—don't let me be normal.

Mary taught me to sight-read. She made me do everything over and over until I could do it seven times in a row, correctly. If you do something seven times in a row correctly, you never forget it, she explained. I've found this to be true, and now I'll repeat "buy eggs, buy eggs, buy eggs, buy eggs, buy eggs, buy eggs, buy eggs" when I'm driving. Sitting at the piano one day, Mary looked at me and ran the back of her pointer finger down my nose.

"You have the most perfect little nose," she said. No one had ever commented on my nose before.

"Thanks," I said.

"Do you do really well in school? I bet you do. I bet you get really good grades."

"Yeah," I lied. Then she had me get on the floor and breathe with a dictionary on my stomach.

Mary taught me not to clench my fists when I sang. How to breathe from my diaphragm. How to use my chest voice and my head voice. How to push my vocal chords close together. Staccato. Legato. We had conversations about my larynx. Mary had her students do a vocal exercise that made you feel beyond ridiculous, especially because her husband taught piano in the next room and his students could hear you.

"who who who! how how how!" she'd have us scream. And then, going down the scale:

"whooooooo, whoooooo, whoo, whoo, whoo, whoo, whoo."

This was a constant sound going on in that yellow house. I heard the girl who had her lesson before me, and the girl waiting for her lesson after me heard me. The girl who took lessons before me, Megan, was three years older than I was, voluptuous and blond, and could *sing*.

Everyone who took lessons with Mary sang Italian arias. I sang "Caro mio ben." "Già il sole dal Gange." "Se tu m'ami." I enjoyed singing these, learning bits of Italian, rolling my Rs. A mustard-yellow book titled *Twenty-Four Italian Songs and Arias of the Seventeenth and Eighteenth Centuries: For Medium High Voice* that I carried around on voice-lesson days was my lifeline.

. . .

"Do you know how to play *anything* on the guitar?" Amanda asked me in high school.

"Nah."

"You'd be cooler if you did," she said.

"I know," I said.

"You should. People would like you more."

I absolutely agreed. It was something I thought about often. My dad was a guitarist. For a long time, to appease people, I'd say, "Yeah, I wish I learned guitar from my dad. Imagine if I had a lesson with my dad every day for my whole life! I'd be an amazing guitarist!" Also, if I played an instrument, I'd have been able to back up my own singing. Then I'd have been able to take my singing further, become more successful.

My friend Kelly and I did take guitar lessons for a hot minute. But we always smoked weed before them and retained nothing. (Some years later we took a bartending class together, smoked weed before it, and retained nothing.) Kelly told me she thought the man teaching us guitar was just looking down our shirts the whole time. We wore such tight and low-cut shirts.

In junior and senior years of high school, Mary sent me to the New York State School Music Association to sing an Italian aria alone in a fluorescent room for three judges. They judged you on posture, diction, intonation, tone, accuracy, and interpretation. After you sang, you sight-read for them. They then scored you (from one to four) and wrote comments to return to your voice teacher. I usually got threes. I didn't mind not excelling. This attitude has gotten me further and allowed me to do more than being a perfectionist would have (like I am right now!). But the competition and scoring turned me off. Being judged wasn't fun but neither was singing for pure enjoyment—a little tortured sounding, maybe, but I never said I wasn't a little tortured.

The summer before senior year of high school, I went to a music camp in Connecticut for two weeks. In my vocal class, we'd all bring in a song, and our coach would accompany us on guitar and give us notes after we sang. I don't remember what I sang, but I remember a girl with auburn hair. When it was her turn, she brought in the Radiohead song "Bullet Proof . . . I Wish I Was." I'd never heard this song before, and I've never since experienced a more moving live performance. She wasn't even standing. (I'd never been allowed to sing without standing.) When she finished, there was a rich silence. We had tears in our eyes. The next time it was her turn, she brought in "Oh! Darling" by the Beatles, and the same thing happened. Maybe that's when I began to give up.

◆　◆　◆

I spent first period in choir through four years of high school while my friends were next door at band. Choir was for slackers. We didn't have to carry instruments, and we could sit there and barely sing and get credit for it. I sang the solo in the choir's performance of Etta James's "At Last." At our senior graduation ceremony, I'd won the choir award, but I was nowhere to be found when they announced my name and called me on stage. I'd ducked out early with my group of pothead friends to smoke blunts and Marlboro Reds.

My poor little lungs.

◆　◆　◆

Nineteen was when I really started to let it all go. I began dating Tim and over dinner at a diner he said, "So what do you like to do? Besides singing?" I didn't know. Smoke? Tim and I smoked lots of weed. Tim mumbled and it rubbed off on me until I was mumbling too. Over-enunciating didn't seem cool anymore.

I am special. I am special. Please, God, please—don't let me be normal! This was the plea deep in my heart, followed by the contrary, *Let me be normal.* That's the difference between child-hood and adolescence. You want to be special as a kid, but as a teenager you want to blend in.

My brother sent me CDs of indie bands he was seeing in Brooklyn. I wondered if I was meant to be in a band like Tilly and the Wall instead of a classical singer. Maybe I was supposed to be like Regina Spektor. Part of the problem was I never found which kind of singer I was supposed to be. I'd grown out of musi-cal theater, wasn't good enough to pursue the arias, wasn't loose or confident enough to be in a band.

When I decided to move to Brooklyn, one of my voice teach-ers (not Mary—another one) gave me a card with a framed photograph of the Williamsburg Bridge. *Keep singing,* she wrote inside.

Everyone was always telling me to keep singing and asking me if I was "still singing" in a way that made me feel very fatigued, even though they probably were just being polite. I felt I always had to justify it if I was not, and if I was, I'd have to tell them what, where, when, and with whom. It did not seem fair that I had to apologize for not pursuing singing. But I brought that *keep singing* card with me through five apartments, hanging it on my fridge. I still have it, hidden in a box.

One day in a grocery store near Mary's house, I turned down the dairy department aisle and saw Mary standing in front of the eggs. I panicked and pivoted, walking as quickly as I could without running, in the opposite direction.

◆ ◆ ◆

My dad and I flew to Berlin together when I was twenty-two to visit my brother. We stayed with Trevor in his flat, and one night after dinner he had some friends over to play music. I overheard my dad and Trevor talking in the kitchen. My dad was saying maybe, hopefully, I'd sing with them later.

"Just see what happens, leave her alone," my brother said.

"Yeah, I know," my dad said.

I was surprised and grateful to hear this conversation. They knew if they pressured me, they would scare me off. I was the monster you couldn't ask to sing anymore. I hadn't realized it was so apparent.

. . .

"I wish I had a talent," I said to my mom one night in the car. We were parked in a church parking lot, waiting for one of my friends. We were listening to an older Rilo Kiley album, and I was singing along.

"Well, you did have a talent, but you decided not to use it," she said.

She didn't say this to hurt my feelings. But I was confused as to how someone made a life out of singing. Sure, I could go to college for it, and then what? I wasn't good enough to go, say, to Juilliard. I would have ended up somewhere like New Paltz or Oneonta, most likely drinking instead of singing.

I'll be thirty soon and haven't taken a voice lesson in a decade. Without understanding why, I gave something up, something I had truly loved. My posture that my teachers had spent years perfecting went to shit, especially when I was drinking. I saw photos of myself hunched over, slouching. When I sing in the car now, I am surprised and embarrassed by how mediocre I sound.

. . .

"I thought you just screwed around with singing, like me," my friend Erika said once.

"No," I replied, snobby. "I *really* sang."

But the more that I don't sing and claim that I used to sing, the more I think my memory of my singing becomes inflated and romanticized.

. . .

Periodically, I've looked up both Heather Rowe and Megan, only to find absolutely nothing. This is the only time I've experienced the disappointment other people feel about me. We couldn't *all* give it up. Especially them, because they were the talented ones I modeled myself after.

◆　◆　◆

I still work occasionally at the music store with my dad. When customers find out I am my father's daughter, they ask me what I play.

"Nothing," I say. This kills the conversation and their faces fall and they look at me with pity.

"I used to sing," I quickly add, to make the conversation go more smoothly, and they perk right back up. Sometimes, depending on the person and the trajectory of the conversation, I pretend I still sing. "I studied voice for ten years," I say. "Italian arias," I offer, and depending on how much I want to fuck with the person, "Opera," I sometimes add, which isn't even true.

◆　◆　◆

The first reading I ever did was at Piano's on Ludlow Street in New York City. I was twenty-five and becoming friends with many writers on Facebook, and now they were clogging up my feed with their photographs of themselves at microphones, holding sheets of paper or their books. Because I did not have a photo of myself at a microphone, I felt self-conscious and inferior. The reading was scheduled months and months ahead, so I approached it as I'd done musical performances or monologues. I took hikes alone and recited my essay out loud until I knew it by heart. I read it in front of the mirror. I could have recited it from memory if the manuscript had been taken away from me. I invited my parents to this reading because I feared it would be the only reading I ever did, ever in my life (though I would go on to do dozens, never practicing, showing up late, showing up on drugs, completely winging it). Before I left for the city, my father came into my bedroom. I was sitting at my desk.

"I'll be о.к., right Dad?" I asked.

"This is the kind of thing you're really good at," he said. I never knew what he meant by that, but I think he meant getting up at a microphone in front of others without having a panic attack.

I overdressed. I wore a fitted red dress and heels like one would wear to the prom. I drove to the city with my friend Kelly, who drank Red Bull and smoked weed on the way. We listened to the Ting Tings and ran out of gas in Bushwick, near the apartment of an ex-boyfriend who hated me. I texted him and asked if I could use his printer (after all that planning, I'd forgotten my pages). He sulked and smoked cigarettes, giving Kelly and me the evil eye the entire time while we changed into our dresses and left.

◆ ◆ ◆

The next day I sat at my desk and looked at photos of myself at the microphone. I was proud; I had joined the club. In the photos, my hands are stiff at my sides. It was uncanny to see that with my posture and half-open mouth and the music stand holding the pages of my essay like sheet music, I looked exactly like all of my singing recital photos. "I look like I'm singing," I said out loud, to an empty room.

Sisterless

"DO YOU GET IN BED and cuddle with Chloe in the mornings?" It was an early evening in spring, and Bobbi and I were in the kitchen, standing across from each other at the counter. We'd just finished eating pizza and salad with ranch on the back porch. Bobbi's mom, Cheryl, was on speakerphone, calling from her hotel to check in on us.

"She doesn't!" I said, making eye contact with Bobbi, who looked at me skeptically in a way only an eight-year-old can.

"Yeah but that's 'cause . . . well, do you sleep naked?" Bobbi asked, lowering her deafening voice for once like she was asking me in total confidence.

I burst out laughing.

"No!" I said.

I've had countless sleepovers with Bobbi in the past three years, and I never don't pretend she's my little sister, even though, at twenty-eight, I'm too old to be her sister. I feel too young and immature to be her mother. At twenty-eight, I'm more like an aunt or a cousin. I could easily be engaged or pregnant or have children of my own. But that is not my life. Instead, I babysit, still waiting for my real life to begin. In limbo. A friend sent me a birthday card that read, *Happy Saturn Return, good luck with that, seriously.*

"You could be in India having sex next year," Cheryl told me once when I was down on myself about being such a loose end in the domestic department.

"Whereas I probably won't!" she said.

When Cheryl called that night, Bobbi and I had been in the middle of an improvised séance, though I was unsure what dead person we were trying to contact. We held hands around an orange candle and chanted gibberish. It reminded me of the opening scene in *Divine Secrets of the Ya-Ya Sisterhood.*

In a mock new-age voice, Bobbi said, "o.k. now breeeeeee-aaathe in the baaaaaad energyyyyyy."

"No way! Not doing that," I said.

"Yeah but then you breathe it out."

"Yeah but why do I have to breathe it in at all?"

"Just trust me and do it."

"K."

"Now look up at the sky and repeat after me: Iloveyoumommy-Iloveyoumommy."

"IloveyoumommyIloveyoumommy."

The phone rang. We screamed.

.   .   .

When I was younger, my mom and I had a running joke about her having another baby. My mother—so youthful at heart—seemed fertile and healthy, in good physical shape, so the joke seemed plausible even when she was in her forties. Once on April Fool's Day many years ago, my mom called up her siblings to lie that she was pregnant, while she and I stifled laughs in the living room. My mom grew up with seven siblings, four sisters and three brothers. I have zero sisters and one brother a couple years older than me. Trevor likes to say we were best friends when we were three and five, but then we didn't talk for years. Then when I was twenty-one and he was twenty-three we became best friends again.

But I couldn't share clothes with a brother. I couldn't ask a brother about my period or my breasts that were getting larger by the day. Sometimes when I was home alone, I would go into my brother's room and try on his jeans. I was envious of him because he had skinny legs and olive skin. I had fair skin and ample legs. I was developing quickly; it seemed more curves appeared each night. I'd go into his room and take his jeans out of his drawers, admire their tininess. The waist four or five inches smaller than my own. The jeans wouldn't fit me, and I'd leave the room defeated and feeling fat.

I begged for a sister. "Let's adopt!" I said. My mom says that since I don't have a sister, my fantasy is better than how it would be in reality. Obviously. In my fantasy we would braid each other's hair and borrow shirts and share cigarettes. Like the scene in *Tiny Furniture* when Lena Dunham is showering and her real-life sister is reading her a poem on the toilet. That would be my life. A little sister. How she'd love me. How I'd love her. We'd speak in our own language and sleep in the same bed. But those are only the cliché things we would do. The real things we would do are too nuanced and special for me to know. I loved *Summer Sisters* by Judy Blume because the girls in it were not blood sisters, and I've spent my life looking for female friendships that would replicate the relationships in that book. I read it three times each summer as a teenager. Beezus and Ramona Quimby. Jessica and Elizabeth Wakefield. Lena and Grace Dunham. Natasha and Malia Obama. Dot and Kit.

• • •

I like to say my father has a thousand daughters. He's had so many teenage girls work at the music store he owns, taught countless girls guitar and ukulele lessons. He's been in some of their lives from when they were seven into their early twenties. The girls still stop by when they're home from college. They leave notes for him on fluorescent Post-its.

Rob, I stopped by but u r avoiding me
i really don't like this distance between us so please be here next time
♥ Sharece
Rob i thought u were my BAE
love ashley

My father has a thousand daughters the way I have a thousand sisters.

• • •

When I was a child, my mother worked for an organization called the Fresh Air Fund. It was a program helping inner-city kids from low-income families to come upstate and stay with a family for a couple of weeks. The year I was six years old, my mother was the chairperson for the Fresh Air Fund. We took the train into Grand Central to pick up the kids and take them back upstate. I brought my blond Baby Alive doll that could eat and poop. My family wasn't getting a "fresh-air kid" that year—we'd hosted one for years, and my dad wanted a summer off from having three children. But on the train home I sat next to a nine-year-old girl. She had a doll too, hers black, mine white. She asked me if she could brush my hair. She brushed and braided it and we played with our dolls. She was outspoken. When we arrived upstate, and the kids went with their corresponding families, Tiffany's family didn't show up.

"I'm going home with YOU! I wanna go with you!" she declared to my mom.

I pleaded, already taken with Tiffany. How do you not love someone who brushes and plays with your hair? I didn't have to twist my mom's arm. We piled in the red Toyota, and Tiffany and I sat thigh to thigh. "cow!" she'd exclaim as we passed farms.

That's how I met Tiffany, my summer sister. She came every summer for the next six years. Tiffany was the funniest person I'd ever met in my short life. Tiffany and I played with American Girl dolls—I had Addy and she had one she'd created that she named Tatiana. She did my hair for years, putting it in elaborate updos and French braids. We shared a bedroom. When we got older, we begged my mom for diaries at Fashion Bug, and we wrote in them at night, griping about each other. *We were SUP-POSED to go the mall but my mom won't take us until Tiffany eats something but she says she's FASTING. SO ANNOYING!!!!*

Every morning, early, my dad would turn on the coffeemaker, and Tiffany told me for the first few years at our house, she didn't know what this sound was. She'd thought it was the sound of my dad farting.

My mother and I recently had a conversation about our summers with Tiffany.

"She brought a lot of laughter to our house when we needed it," she said. My parents were still together then, but there were issues. Such as my dad coming home to find he had an extra child in the living room, one with a booming laugh, brushing his daughter's hair.

We brought Tiffany to Cape Cod with us one summer. We jumped the waves. Tiffany borrowed my mom's turquoise two-piece suit, and she got wrecked from a wave, laughing and crying, her bikini top falling off. Tiffany was vocal about hating mosquitos, sun, grass, swimming. When we were kids, my brother and I played outside in the sandbox. My mom told her to play with us.

"I'm not getting in that! That's *dirt*!" she said.

◆ ◆ ◆

I've always idolized older girls. Even now some of my best friends are in their forties. There's a photo of Tiffany and me where she is crossing her legs, so I am too. Besides Tiffany, I also had my cousin Megan for a surrogate big sister. Megan was five years older than me, my cool cousin—skinnier, blonder, older. I got my belly button pierced because hers was. I got my cartilage pierced because hers was (she took me). I waitressed because she did, drove stick shift because she did. When I was a freshman in high school, she was a freshman in college, at SUNY. My parents had just separated, and Megan e-mailed me to invite me to stay with her for a weekend. I brought my two best friends along. I forever jokingly blame this experience for why I did not go to college. It was the first time I funneled beer, and my friends and I ended up throwing up all over the place. Megan lent me her expired ID, and I bought beer with it from ages sixteen to nineteen, when my mom found it while snooping through my jeans. She mailed it back to Megan with a note saying, *There are other ways to be a cool cousin.*

Megan warned me about getting older. Every year since I've turned twenty-five, on my birthday she reminds me, "It's all downhill from here." We went to the beach every summer, and we once saw a woman with tan legs, loose skin wobbling all around. "I'm scared my legs are gonna look like *that*," she said. Another year we walked along the water and she said, "My thighs rub together while I walk now. They never used to do that." It was one of the most morbid statements I've ever heard, and it still haunts me. I was twenty-three then and assumed my body would function perfectly my entire life. Now my thighs also rub together.

Megan and I spent this past New Year's Eve together.

"Remember when you wanted a breast reduction?" I asked her over a glass of champagne.

"Yeah, now I want a lift," she responded.

. . .

The first time I met Bobbi was in 2011, when she was five and I was twenty-five. She was always animated, but polite and somewhat shy. (Now that we are pseudo-sisters, now that she is ten, she is not polite and shy with me. Sometimes I have to tell her to give me ten minutes. Sometimes I have to take her into the other room. Sometimes we yell and I swear.)

In 2013 I lived at Cheryl's during the months of November and December while her family went to Australia. It was just me and her two cats in the house. The house was medium-sized but felt big for only one person. I was lonely. I knew I wasn't a child anymore, but I didn't know myself as an adult yet, either. Instead of sleeping in the main bedroom, I found myself over and over retiring to Bobbi's small bed on the floor, with the red-and-blue Spider-Man fleece blanket. Last year I told Bobbi I slept in her bed instead of her mom's so I could curl up next to the wall.

"That is the *weirdest* thing I've ever heard in my whole life," she said.

. . .

Last summer I stayed with Bobbi and her older brother, Carver, in Portland for a week, and there was an E. coli scare. We had to boil and bottle the water before we drank it. The kids were excited because they got to drink Gatorade and Vitaminwater and sugary drinks they normally weren't allowed to have. It was all anyone was talking about. E. coli. One morning at the dog park with Bobbi's puppy, Janie, Bobbi asked me, "What would you do if there wasn't any water to drink for a month?"

I said I would go in grocery stores and suck water from different fruits and that I would go to parks in the early morning and lick the dew off the grass. Bobbi burst into hysterics, like this was the most ridiculous thing she'd ever heard.

"I would just make *smoothies!*" she exclaimed. And then, "Do you think Janie knows what she looks like? Like, do you think she thinks she's a really good-looking dog?"

◆　◆　◆

Bobbi is passionate about horror. She gets a rush from scaring herself crapless. She loves true stories and ghost stories and the author April Henry. One afternoon we drove to Powell's, where I promised to buy her one book. She had to make the excruciatingly difficult decision between April Henry's novels *The Body in the Woods* and *Girl, Stolen*. She chose *The Body in the Woods*. She sleeps in her brother's room the nights she binges on horror. She'll follow me everywhere, saying things like, "What if we open the door and there's a serial killer sitting at the table?" and "What if we come upon a dead clown?" She wants desperately not to be alone after reading these books and watching these movies. She even comes into the bathroom with me and stands under a bath towel while I pee. But she's addicted.

◆　◆　◆

One day we were in her mom's library looking at the books on the shelves. I pointed out my book of essays.

"What's it about?" Bobbi asked.

"My life."

She grew uncharacteristically quiet.

"Was your life sad?"

"No . . ." I said.

She perked back up and matter-of-factly said, "Good!"

"Why?" I asked.

"Because when people write about their lives, they usually had bad or sad lives."

"That's a great observation," I said.

◆ ◆ ◆

I get irritated in the mornings packing Bobbi's lunches when she didn't eat the tomato soup she'd begged me to put into a Thermos and the hummus and pita and apple and orange I packed the day before. She only ate the two Thin Mints. I toss it all into the compost and ask Bobbi why she didn't eat at lunchtime.

"I was too busy talking and telling ghoooossssst stories!" she said.

"Well, try to eat what I pack you today, 'cause this is a waste of food and a waste of my time."

"*Yes, ma'am!*" she shouted, dramatically straightening her posture and hand-saluting me.

"Can I try your coffee, pleeeeeeaaase? Can you give me your iPhone password, pleeeeeeeaaaaassse?"

"I'm so happy you're seeing how hard my life is," Cheryl said that day and gave me a gift certificate to Massage Envy.

In my own life, in my own apartment, all I have to take care of is a jade plant, which barely needs anything. Besides that I just make sure to get out of bed every day, shower, eat protein, get a little exercise. I answer to no one. So it's a trip, walking into Cheryl's and having responsibility for not only two small humans but also a dog and two cats and a fish. Usually I am my first priority, but now I am my last. When evening rolls around, I become completely overwhelmed with fixing dinner, loading the dishwasher, walking the dog, getting the kids to brush their teeth. I often pass out right after they do, not enough energy to finish a glass of wine or read one of Cheryl's one million books and advance review copies.

I am asked if I have children only once or twice a year, and I try not to bristle. I'm not exactly sure why I do bristle—I think because these people are not really seeing me, seeing my incredibly non-mom life. I try not to scream, like in that episode of *Broad City*, I AM NOT A MOM! DO I LOOK LIKE I HAVE KIDS?

I've noticed for the past few years, I've been trying on families instead of boyfriends. Through writing I've made many special friendships with women in their forties. There is one decade between us, and I'm curious what that decade will make of me. I visit these women, stay at their homes with their husbands and children. I sleep in their guest rooms or their daughters' beds. I observe. I note-take in my mind. *I want open communication the way they have, but I don't want a rescue dog because I won't be able to juggle a kid and a dog.* They have what I do not—stability, Legos, school lunches—and I have what they do not: endless time to read or masturbate or watch three movies in a row or stare at the ceiling wondering what is to become of them.

· · ·

In her essay "Munro Country" about her infatuation with author Alice Munro, Cheryl writes, "I didn't *really* think I was Alice Munro's daughter. I'm not talking here about delusion."

I feel similarly about Bobbi. I don't *actually* think she is my sister. I'm just joking around. But it would be untrue to say I don't feel a connection. When we lie on the couch watching *Bob's Burgers*, my feet in Bobbi's lap, when we walk down the street and she puts her arm around my waist, when she wakes me up in the middle of the night to get her water, or when she animatedly tells me about her dreams over tea and eggs in the mornings, I feel safe. Something akin to love.

· · ·

When I made friends with Fran, she was someone I recognized immediately as family. It was as though I'd known her forever. She was so familiar to me and I couldn't fathom it.

"I can't believe how well we get along," I said to her. "This is crazy."

"Maybe we're karmic sisters," she responded. "That happens sometimes."

＋　＋　＋

Bobbi and I watched *My Girl*. "This is my new favorite movie," she declared. We watched *The Sisterhood of the Traveling Pants*. We watched *Anchorman 2. Mean Girls 2. The Sandlot 2. Zoolander 2*. We ate at Red Robin. We ordered pizza and Caesar salad and went out for cheeseburgers. We went on the tire swing at the park. We did yoga on the front porch. We drew pictures. We went to the pet store for materials to clean her fish tank. We picked flowers. I practiced her lines with her when she got the part of Elsa in her acting class's version of *Frozen*. Her best friend came over and they danced on top of the coffee table to "Call Me Maybe." I drove Bobbi and Carver to school, piano class, acting class, soccer, and basketball practice. I sat on the bench while she participated in her parkour class. "Are you gonna stay and watch?" she'd asked me.

One thing I love about kids is they don't even know how much they are helping you. The summer I had a broken heart so bad I thought I was dying, Taylor Swift's song "Trouble" had just been released. We were in the car all the time, as the children's camps were opposite directions from one another. "Trouble" came on the radio often, and each time, Bobbi and I sang it at the top of our lungs. I call this sort of thing "active grieving."

I knew you were trouble when you walked in
So shame on you now
Flew me to places I've never been
Now I'm lying on the cold, hard floor

Carver told us our singing was really annoying. He asked me to please change the station.

During the breakup, I showed up to babysit and told Cheryl I was in a bad headspace. That I was devastated. "Is it terrible or will you be o.k.?" she asked. I was about to tell her it was terrible, and I wouldn't o.k., but she interrupted and said, "Listen—even if it is terrible, you will be o.k. And if it makes you feel any better—my twenties were full of crazy bitches."

. . .

If you ask kids, "Wanna do something fun?" they yell, "Yeah!" Adults don't do this. They often roll their eyes and groan, "Like what?"

On my last day with Bobbi before I would fly back to New York, I picked her up at school. I loved picking her up in the afternoons, feeling like anything was possible. The sun shone on the windshield. Bobbi saw me from the distance and jumped in the car.

"Hi, friend," I said.

"Hi, friend!"

"Let's have fun!"

"Yeah! Let's get frozen yoooooooogurt!" she said.

"Good idea!"

"Guess what a boy gave me," she said, pulling a large chocolate bar wrapped in gold foil out of her backpack.

I'd been craving chocolate all day.

"I love you so much right now," I said, reaching my hand back for a piece.

"Yay," she said, slapping a square in my hand.

We parked on Hawthorne Boulevard and skipped around town. We got frozen yogurt. While I was in the bathroom, Bobbi piled her yogurt with everything I said she couldn't have, like gummy bears and chocolate chips. We went to the bookstore. We went to one of my favorite boutiques because I had babysitting money burning a hole in my pocket. She helped me pick out a jean jacket with sweatshirt sleeves. I rolled the sleeves up, and she said, "No, keep 'em down, that's how the kids are wearing them." I got a text from Cheryl, *Coming home soon?* We jumped back into the car, singing along to First Aid Kit on the *Wild* soundtrack.

"Are you thinking about mac and cheese?" Bobbi asked me as I drove, catching my eye in the rearview mirror.

"No . . ."

"Oh. You look like you are."

. . .

Two summers ago, Cheryl was teaching a writing workshop at Omega Institute for a couple of weeks, and my mom and I drove there to have dinner with Cheryl's family. We opened a bottle of red and a bottle of white and ate cheese and crackers.

"You guys—do you know the story of how we know Chloe and her mom?" Cheryl asked her kids.

"Yep," Bobbi said, coming to sit next to me on the couch and patting me twice on the knee.

"You do? What is it?" Cheryl asked, sipping her wine.

"Like—we're actually all related or something," Bobbi said dismissively, shoving crackers into her mouth, already bored by the story.

"What did she say?" my mom asked me from across the room.

"She said we're all related."

My mom and Cheryl and I laughed. We told the story, which is a complicated one with a few twists.

In spring of 2011, I'd just begun publishing my writing online, and I published an essay on the *Rumpus*. The anonymous writer Dear Sugar commented, *Chloe Caldwell, I don't know who you are, but I know you're a sweet pea rock star. I loved this essay. Loved it. Keep on writing like a motherfucker, sister.* I was touched but had no clue who this mysterious writer was. I thanked her on Twitter.

Meanwhile, I was sitting on my mom's couch reading personal essays in the *Sun* magazine online. I stumbled upon "The Love of My Life" and was so moved I called my mom into the room and told her she had to read it. My mom looked over my shoulder and said, "I think I've read that. I think I even e-mailed the author." This habit of e-mailing authors when they make you feel something is one of the best traits my mother has passed down to me.

I messaged Cheryl on Twitter telling her I loved her essay, and she told me she loved my *Rumpus* essays. We began e-mailing. I was e-mailing with both Dear Sugar and Cheryl Strayed at this point and had no idea they were the same person.

I told Cheryl my mom thought she'd e-mailed her many years ago. Cheryl responded four minutes later:

Is your mother Michele? She e-mailed me in 2002. We had an exchange about how much we both love Lucinda Williams. How old were you then?

Sixteen. I was sixteen then, and here I was eleven years later, unknowingly e-mailing the same author about the same essay my mother had.

That same spring, I got a book deal for my first book. All of these magical things were happening. *Did Cheryl do this?* I wondered. I asked her.

"I didn't say anything to anyone," she said. "It was all you, babe. In some interesting way, it was your mother who brought us together, through my mother. They were the original contact. I wrote in the *Sun* about how much I loved my mother, and *your* mother wrote to me saying she loved it. Our friendship was in the stars."

◆　◆　◆

After dinner in the cafeteria at Omega—including a vegan cup-cake we all found inedible—we took a walk on one of the trails to a pond. Bobbi was licking my arm.

"Give me some space," I said.

"Yeah, *God*, Bobbi, why do you get so hyper around Chloe? It's annoying," her brother said.

"Because she's awesome," Bobbi said.

On this fifteen-minute walk, Bobbi wanted me to give her dares.

"Run to that tree and do twenty jumping jacks."

"o.к. now what?"

"Say, 'Hi, how are you?' to this group of boys walking toward us."

"o.к. now what?"

"Count to one hundred."

"o.к. now what?"

"Stop talking to me for one full minute."

"Oh *come on.*"

⋆　⋆　⋆

When I stay with Bobbi consecutive nights, we become so used to each other we finish each other's sentences. When I accidentally broke the family's SodaStream bottle, she wrote an apology note to her parents, from me. When she got lice, I shampooed her hair. I sat on the toilet while she bathed, and we talked about the girls in her class. Her dog and kitten sat with us in the bathroom. She wears my т-shirts a few days in a row. She gets the shirt dirty and documents everything we did on it. "This is when we ate ice cream at Salt and Straw, this is when we painted pictures . . ." She wears my band shirt that says *Girls In Trouble.* "Next time you come," she said, "can you bring me a shirt that says *Tomboy* on it?" After meeting my mom a couple of times, she once said, "Your mom's, like, *active.*"

"What do you mean?" I asked.

"You know, like, she's a 'let's have a dance party' kind of person," she explained impatiently. "And she photo bombs people."

⋆　⋆　⋆

When Cheryl had to fly to Los Angeles to attend the Golden Globes, she flew me to Portland to stay with her kids for a week. The kids and I had a Golden Globes party. We ordered pizzas and I broke out the wine with my friends. Every time we saw Cheryl on the тv screen, we screamed.

"Be *quiet*, everybody!" Bobbi said, jumping up and running to the TV to see her mother. "She might *say* something about us!"

When we picked Cheryl back up from the airport, the first thing Bobbi said was, "Chloe said 'fuck' seven times driving here."

"Did you say 'fuck' seven times?" Cheryl turned her head to look at me.

• • •

Bobbi and I both eat avocados out of the shell with lots of salt. I know she likes her eggs scrambled hard, and she knows I get lost if she's engaging me in a conversation while I drive. She taught me frozen blueberries are delicious in oatmeal, and I taught her what the word *stealth* means. Sometimes we buy candles and she runs and drops them on my friends' doorsteps. We both have a love affair with macaroni and cheese. We love nonfiction books and don't care for sports. When we walk to the store for butter at night because we don't have any to make chocolate chip cookies, I am surprised to see she does what I do when I'm alone—when she sees a man walking toward us, she crosses the street to the other side. "He's freaky," she says, grabbing my hand.

When I fly home after my weeklong babysitting stints, I always feel melancholy. I lament I was too hard on her—not fun enough, too strict, and I ache for her company. I miss the height of her standing next to me at all times, especially when we brush our teeth or cook meals, her head near my shoulders. I open my computer and find she'd been looking up the ten worst shark attacks on YouTube.

I miss you, I texted her from the airport. *Hi I miss you too*, she texted back, along with every single emoji that exists. It must have taken at least an hour. Cheryl texted me the next day, *Sorry Bobbi sent you one thousand emojis! She only did it because she loves you.*

I know she does, I said.

PART 3

The Girls of My Youth

THE FIRST GIRL I LOVED lived up the street from me; it was super convenient. Her parents wrote for *Parents* magazine. Sara was the first person I experienced different feelings and emotions on and for, and the first human I knew outside of my family. She loved me back, still does. We went to preschool (pee-school, we called it) together. We carpooled to school together through ninth grade, when her parents sent her to a private school. (That was the year all my best girl friends were sent to private schools, and I was left with male friends.) In the beginning, you're friends with someone because they live up the street from you. This is why life gets so complicated later, when you have the freedom to actually fall in love with anyone—regardless of how close their street is to yours.

When we were six years old, we played house in a super-sexy way. We'd shut the door to her bedroom or mine and straddle and hump each other. That's how I learned to orgasm. I don't actually think I had orgasms back then, I just knew it felt good. A friend once found out I masturbated only on my stomach and she mused out loud it was interesting how I have to "ride to come." I blame Sara and our game.

The game should have more accurately been called "Sex House." We knew what we were doing was only for closed doors, because once in my room, when my father entered without knocking, we jumped off of each other and yelled, "WE'RE TAKING A NAP!"

Another game we liked to play was one where we read our separate books next to each other and only read the dialogue parts out loud. On a Sunday night we did this in the hammock.

"Honey, it's Sunday," I said, because that's what was in my book, and we laughed until we cramped and cried.

Sara and I shared the talent of hearing a song once and knowing the song's words forever. We especially loved Lou Bega,
Christina Aguilera, and LeAnn Rimes. At her new high school
in Massachusetts, Sara met a girl named Lily. She was blond like
me and we shared a birthday and they became best friends. We
sent some hurt e-mails back and forth—her e-mail address was
Juniormint09@angelfire.com. I hung out with them a few times,
Sara's sweet attempt at trying to make me part of it, her attempt to
make me love Lily too, but best friends rarely come in threes and
eventually we both let go. I still see photos of them together on
Facebook and get tense. Sara is the one person in my life who, aside
from my parents, has wished me happy birthday every single year.

My second best friend was Sarah with an *h*. We met in fourth grade.
She is most remembered for the time she jerked off her dog Marlo
in front of everyone with a plastic baggie over her hand. Later she
denied denied denied. Sarah and I were cruel. We were mean girls.
We wrote notes to each other that said things like, *Sabrina's shirt is
really ugly . . . let's tell her it's a really nice shirt and she should wear it
all the time.* Sarah lived in a trailer (a detail I found glamorous and
cozy), and I slept there on both Friday and Saturday nights sometimes. I went to church with her family on Sundays, which I loved,
since my family didn't go to church. We ate cheeseballs at night
and watched *I Love Lucy*, which I loved, since my family didn't
buy cheeseballs or have cable. She loved horror, and I pretended
to. We watched *Scream* and *Scream 2* and *I Know What You Did
Last Summer*. Sarah and I thought pot was just mixed herbs, so
we rolled joints of oregano and smoked them, thinking we were
getting high. We practiced kissing on our hands and compared the
growth of our breasts. I lent her this Sally Hansen hair removal
cream that she used on her mustache. The next day she was so
mad, "I can't believe you let me use that! I broke out and had a red
mustache! I looked like a clown! I'm going to kill you."

I remember waking up one Sunday morning in my bed with
Sarah to the radio playing—we'd left it on through the night.
On Casey Kasem's Top Forty, the new Sheryl Crow song "My

Favorite Mistake" played. I was thinking how much I loved this new song when Sarah said, "My favorite mistake? This song is soooooooooo gay." Sarah with an *h* once called Sara without an *h* "Matzah Breath."

At my twelfth birthday party, I had five girls over, and we played girl-on-girl spin the bottle. It's not that my parents were strict and didn't allow boys; it just ended up being that way. After we all kissed (I had braces) we wanted to watch the movie *Clueless*. Sarah with an *h* had to call her parents for permission, and they said no.

Sarah, Sara, and I were all dressing the same at thirteen. Individuality was way too terrifying. We wanted to look like tomboys. We spent our birthday and Christmas money and allowances at Abercrombie & Fitch, only able to afford the sale T-shirts that read *Abercrombie* on them. We wore baggy jeans from Pacific Sunwear, hemp chokers, and navy blue polo shirts. We styled our hair in buns. Sneakers: Vans, Airwalks, Sketchers. We were always having dramatic conflicts and crying and bringing one another to the guidance counselor's office.

Mary and I had known each other since elementary school, but it wasn't until we were fourteen that we developed a real chemistry, a similar sense of humor. Mary had a pool with a diving board and a ping-pong table and took piano lessons in the mornings with a guy named Mr. Claus—he was a large man with a white beard too. Any house with two bathrooms was insanity to me, and Mary's house had three bathrooms. I loved singing "Shabbat Shalom" at her dinner table and lighting the menorah. We called into radio stations and requested the song "Do You Really Want Me" by Robyn. We spent hours straightening our naturally thick and curly hair. When that high-end straightener, the Chi, came out, our lives were changed. We saved up fifty dollars to buy one. Mary and I shaved our legs for the first time sitting on her bathroom counter together, giddy at the smoothness. We listened to the song "That Thing You Do!" all the time after seeing the movie. Mary, like Sara, went away for high school. But we didn't lose touch—instead, I became friends with all her friends, and she included me in everything.

At fourteen, Amy, Kelly, and I became obsessed with the movie *Gia*, starring Angelina Jolie. We liked her mouth, her skin, her tits. At a sleepover at my friend Amy's trailer, we snuck out and went pool hopping and drank beers we took from her mom's fridge. When we got back, we were muddy, and Amy threw us in the bathtub. Amy fingered our friend Kelly or vice versa; my memory of it is vague. Then we would lie in bed and cut out photos of Angelina to make collages. In the morning, Kelly said, "Why do Jewish girls get to look so pretty in the morning?" Even then, we hated our skin. Too white. There's a photograph of me from that morning with a black eye, curled up on Kelly's shoulder. A boy had thrown a snowball at me and hit me in the face.

My last name and Kelly's begin the same way, so we grew up shoulder to shoulder. We were next to each other for everything: lockers, desks, the line for the bus. Teachers were on to us and would sit a goody-two-shoes boy in between us, like Frank Morris or Ryan Silver. We'd imitate Frank's noisy mouth-breathing or stroke our feet against Ryan's legs, attempting to give him a boner in front of everyone. Sometimes after school, we kissed in the community center in the coatroom because the older boys would pay us five or ten dollars. We needed the money so we could go tanning. Sometimes we went into churches and threw water on one another's heads, "baptizing" each other. We stole lipstick from Rite Aid. We failed math class, and our teacher put Kelly in the back of the room alone at a desk, telling her she was in "Siberia." We loved reading, and we stole books from our classrooms: *To Kill a Mockingbird*, *The Diary of Anne Frank*, *Ordinary People*. Kelly and I grew tits before everyone else did. We were the same size but completely different shapes. Hers were round and mine were pointy. We shared every single one of our shirts: tight short-sleeve scoop necks and v-necks. Kelly's older brothers had huge jars of homegrown weed, and we'd steal handfuls and smoke it but also give it away. Boys loved hanging out with us until we stole their money or their weed, and then they hated us. My dad drove us five hours to Ithaca so we could see No Doubt. He always tells me when he went to pick us up, he thought to himself, *I'll just look for the two girls dressed like sluts.* I don't remember ever dressing as a slut, but I guess we did wear skintight clothing. My dad thought it was funny Kelly ate only white foods, and he'd adhere to her diet and make us gnocchi with white cream sauce. We liked taking three kinds of cereal and mixing them into a big pot to eat all at once. At seventeen when we drove to Planned Parenthood for STD tests and I was sure I had something, Kelly said, "You won't have one. Only *good* people get those."

Amy was the most sexually adventurous of us all. Kelly loves remembering, "When Amy got her period, she just went into the bathroom and stuck a tampon up herself." Unlike the rest of us (me), who were afraid. Amy would meet boys and let them finger her. Unlike the rest of us (me), she wasn't afraid sex would hurt and lost her virginity years before I did. She took her clothes off easily. She went swimming anywhere. We ate ecstasy and drove around, singing to Macy Gray and Ben Folds Five. We got drunk on Rolling Rock before school. She was school-smart, and I cheated off her in French class. "How are you going to function without Chloe?" our government teacher once asked her. "You not having Chloe's like . . . not having your finger," he said. We sometimes kissed with tongues at parties. My boyfriend John took a photo of us French kissing and kept it on his minifridge for years. When I slept at Amy's after parties, I'd ask her to put ice cream in a bowl and microwave it for me.

Freshman and sophomore years of high school Kelly and I were dressing the same again, but now it was super-tight and low-cut shirts and jeans our mothers said looked like we "poured ourselves into." Our hair was getting blonder, our breasts getting bigger, our lipstick getting darker, and our skin getting tanner. Our grades were getting worse. The school was always freezing, and our hard nipples showed through our shirts. We started sweating and had wet circles underneath our armpits.

The man I loved the most wasn't a woman, but when I compare him to other men, I realize he was womanly. My girl friends would meet him and text me later saying, *I like him, but wow, he was so effeminate.* He was overly enthusiastic. He made up songs about caterpillars. He sang along to my *Beauty and the Beast* soundtrack in the car. He cried passionately and often. He read me his journals while we were in bed. He was nostalgic and obsessive and regretful. He was embarrassingly honest and loud. He was exhaustive. We were too alike. No one liked being around us at the same time.

"You're both manic-like," my mom always said. "You're grandiose around each other." He told me I was the woman he would want to be if he were a woman.

"Why are you *so* sensitive!" he yelled to me from the bathroom once.

"Because I am!" I yelled. "Why are you?"

He walked into the bedroom and looked into my eyes. I had bolted upright on the bed. I looked into his shining eyes and we both laughed.

"Because I am," he said calmly.

Sara without an *h* and I are still friends. It seems our love is unconditional. I recently visited her in Denver, where she owns a small dog and takes Ubers. I never saw Sarah with an *h* again after high school. I can't remember the last time I saw Mary, but I run into her mother once a year at restaurants. Kelly lives a few blocks away from me with her boyfriend, and we still share dresses and shirts. Amy lives forty-five minutes away and has a two-year-old baby. Fifteen years ago we were kissing in twin beds on acid, now we're turning thirty, hungover from two drinks, worrying about spider veins and broken capillaries.

The other day, Amy came over after her gynecologist appointment. The gyno had asked her if she'd ever had an abnormal pap smear.

"I know it sounds either like I'm lying or I'm really stupid," she'd answered, "but I honestly can't remember if it was me . . . or if it was my friend."

The Laziest Coming Out Story
You've Ever Heard

+ My friend Lauren told me her number on the Kinsey scale
  went up this year after reading my book *Women*, which
  is about a lesbian love affair, and after watching Allison
  Williams play Peter Pan in *Peter Pan Live*.

+ Another friend, Renee, e-mailed me: *Zach had heard I'm
  now open to dating women and he was like, "So what does that
  mean, what are you doing to meet women and date?" and I was
  like, "Oh literally nothing, I'm just like, inwardly identifying as
  queer now and am now open to being seduced by anyone, male
  or female." "That is the laziest coming out story I've ever heard,"
  he said.*

+ I told Renee I would be using that anecdote in an essay. I
  asked her if she wanted me to use her name, or call her "a
  friend." She replied, "A friend. I'm not out yet."

+ "*Everyone's* bisexual!" This was me and my friend Kelly's
  party trick in middle school through high school. It riled
  people, and we knew it. And by *people*, I mean males. They
  laughed in our faces, thinking it ridiculous.

+ After my first relationship with a woman, I talked to Kelly
  on the phone. "*Everyone's* bisexual, remember?" she said.

+ Ashley Ford interviewed me over the phone for Buzzfeed
  LGBT. To have the abbreviation LGBT even associated with
  my name is odd to me. I never came out as bisexual. I just
  wrote a book with a narrator who is confused around her
  sexuality. I asked Ashley why it was important to her to have
  B for Bisexual in her Twitter bio. She explained because even
  though she's in a relationship with a man, it's still part of her.
  I asked her about her coming out.

+ "I never came out, I just started writing about it."
+ "Me too," I told her.
+ Which begs the question: is that a cop out? Someone told me it was brave. I disagree. I told her it felt passive aggressive. "I guess we're thinking about it in different ways," she said.
+ The end of the Buzzfeed article quotes me saying, "I'm o.k. with [the label] bisexual." It makes me cringe. I have issues with labels, yet don't know what to do without them.
+ When you label me, you negate me. Either that or I'm a coward with intimacy issues.
+ I understand it is 2016 now. I understand it was 100 percent more difficult in all of the previous years. I understand I am lucky. I understand because of Ellen DeGeneres and Ellen Page and *The L Word* and Leslie Feinberg, things are different. I also understand distress and confusion are the same regardless of what year it is.
+ After sleeping with a woman for the first time, I felt like I was dying. My life was the t.a.t.u song, "All the Things She Said." *I'm in serious shit, I feel totally lost, if I'm asking for help, it's only because being with you has opened my eyes.* The song's World Public Library entry reads "The song's lyrics are about the relationship between the two girls, how each is continually in the other's thoughts, with the themes relating to homosexuality, bisexuality, and love."
+ One of the best parts about the show *Broad City* is the nonchalant way the character Ilana likes both men and women without it being a *thing*.
+ We are in a culture of noncommitment. We end our sentences with "idk" and "or whatever" and "idgi." But we are still not allowed this in the sexuality department. Straight, gay, or bi? idk. idgi.
+ icymi: I'm confused about my sexuality.
+ Eating pho with my friend Amanda on First Avenue, she says, "So you're not bisexual but you're not straight?" "Yeah," I say. She looks up from her noodles and says, "I don't understand, like, anything about you."

+ I do not consider myself a political person. I never have been.
  A female author—I cannot remember who—once wrote
  something like, "I'm not political in my writing, why should
  I be? If you look at my life, I'm political in the way I live." It
  comforted me to no end. I do not watch the news. I read a
  little. I'm too sensitive for it and too dumb. But when I read
  that, I thought, *Yeah!* I don't talk about women writers needing to be read, but I wrote a book that didn't have any men
  in it without even noticing. Not tooting my own horn here,
  expressing my naiveté.

+ On Instagram, someone I don't know posted a photo of my
  book *Women* and wrote, *I was really stoked to read a book
  about bisexual curiosities—bisexuality often gets ignored in our
  black-and-white world. Unfortunately Caldwell never really
  touches on the wide and varied spectrum of sexuality—though
  this was just something that I wanted, but by no means do I think
  she is beholden to being a voice for bisexual politics.*

+ My friend jokes she has a Google alert for "bisexual celebrities" on her computer.

+ On OkCupid, a person named Randall messaged me.
  Randall didn't have a photo, but seemed cool. We switched
  over to e-mail, and Randall sent a photograph. She wasn't the
  attractive woman I'd imagined, but a thirty-something male,
  playing with his nephew. *I think my profile says I'm looking
  for women,* I wrote. *Me too, lol,* he responded.

+ On OkCupid, a woman asked me, "So you're bisexual, but
  you're on the women tip right now?"

+ While I was in a relationship with a woman, I went to a
  Fourth of July party. At the end of the night, I was walking
  to my car with some people I didn't know, including a gay
  man. He'd been trying to meet men that night and was frustrated on his luck. "No one's gay," he griped. "*Everyone's gay!*"
  I said, excited about my newfound sexuality. "That's easy
  for a straight white woman to say," he said.

+ When I think of this now, I try to tell myself I stayed quiet.
  I feel shame about speaking up, for some reason or another.

I feel bad for making him feel bad—how very female. I smiled. I was shocked, because I was so changed on the inside but not on the outside. I was wearing a dress and had long hair. "You think I'm straight," I said. He was embarrassed. He started apologizing.

+ I've always been interested in how we can look one way and be something else entirely. Now, I was getting tired of it.

+ My "out" friend wore shirts that read *Legalize Gay. Maybe I should do that*, I'd always think to myself when I saw her wearing them.

+ How many times have I done the same thing? Assume a woman straight, only to be so thrown when she mentions having dated a woman.

+ It's so exciting when this happens. "Can you believe it?" I'll say to people. No one is ever what they seem, yet it's not as exciting to be like, "Can you believe it, her favorite color is red—I thought it was green!" Or, "She's from Texas, I thought she was from New York City!"

+ My mom used to have a bumper sticker tacked up by our calendar in the hallway that said, *Don't Believe Everything You Think.* "I don't get it," I whined for years.

+ And the opposite. In a video when Lena Dunham interviews Miranda July, July tells Dunham about being at Vipassana (a ten-day silent meditation retreat) and becoming besotted with a woman there. At the retreat, the participants were not allowed to speak or make eye contact or even facial expressions. They all wore the same thing, black pants and shirts. July was positive her crush was a "powerful butch woman." "I wanted her fingers inside me," she says. On the last day of Vipassana, they changed out of their black sweats. July was excited to talk to this woman and see if their connection was, in fact, real. The woman came out of her cabin wearing mom jeans, a pink polo shirt, and white tennis sneakers and hopped into her minivan with her husband. July joked she was devastated. The moral of the story is, according to July, "If you wanted it badly enough, you could completely

misread someone as a lesbian." "So it's like, if you want it
badly enough, you could mistake anyone for someone you
could love," Dunham says. "Right," July says. "Or a lesbian,"
Dunham says. They laugh. "It was a confusing time for me,"
July says.

+ We all want to judge but don't want to be judged.

+ I published a version of this essay online and some girl
tweeted, LOL *at basics figuring out they're bisexual but it's none
of my business.* I was livid and tweeted back, *Yeah, that's a
pretty immature and rude thing to say.* She favorited my tweet.
I muted her. Someone told me to take that anecdote out of
this essay. "She wins that way," they said. I don't care.

+ My therapist once set me up so I was forced to say "I could be
with a woman" and "I could be with a man" out loud. "Well,
when I say it *that* way, it's not a big deal," I said.

+ Last summer, my mother and I were cleaning out my apartment on the same day as the Pride parade. We took a break
and walked to the parade. My dad was there too. The three
of us stood in silence. It meant something to me, since I
was inwardly identifying as queer now. *Maybe they know,* I
thought.

+ A few weeks after, my mom and I took a walk, and she told
me about an old coworker of hers. She'd looked her up on
Facebook and was surprised to see she'd married a butch-
looking woman. My mom said she looked happy and that she
was happy for her. "That's the whole story?" I asked. She said
it was. "That's a nice story, Mom," I said.

+ I stayed a night at the St. Marks Hotel with a girl friend
from high school. In the morning she kept calling me "weird"
because the night before I hooked up with a girl. *Weird.
You're weird.* I got pissed, picking a fight with her later via
text. *I say "weird" because I'm being lazy,* she said. *I'll work on
getting better at saying what I mean. I guess like, "weird" as in,
different than what I do maybe?*

+ Once a girl friend who I'd been intimate with said, while
lying in bed, "Oh, Chloe. You're an alien." As much as this

scared me, some part of me took it as a compliment. But mostly it did scare me. I'm an alien. I will never have a sexual identity. I will never have a normal life. I should have asked her what she meant.

+ Having dinner with my friend Karina, she's like, "The more kinds of gay people and the more ways of being gay, the better!"

+ When I walk by men, my thought process goes, *Don't fucking look at me, I'm just trying to walk down the street in a dress, do not fucking talk to me, why aren't you looking at me, aren't I attractive, ugh, I knew it, men think I'm ugly.*

+ In her book *My Life as a Dyke*, Erika Kleinman writes about dating a woman who liked to say, "I don't date fucking bisexuals, because they don't fucking exist."

+ Erika has told me, "I'm married to a man, but I could have easily married a woman since I'm completely bisexual. I am a Kinsey 3! Seriously, if someone asks me about my sexual orientation, I'm like, 'Depends. Who's asking?' Oh look, there's a lesbian couple over there. Or maybe they're sisters. Whatever, the one with the white streak in her hair and the Escher tat is fucking hot."

+ In the movie *Appropriate Behavior*, writer and actress Desiree Akhavan tells her brother she's dating a woman. "So you're gay now?" "Well, I like dating men too, so I guess I'm bisexual," she responds. "That's a thing?" he asks. "I'm afraid so," she says.

+ At a bar one night, I sat on the patio with a friend from high school. "You're not bisexual," he said, "you're just trying to be cool."

+ Later on in our conversation, he said, "You could date a girl? Marry a girl?" and looks relatively disgusted. "Sure," I said. "Couldn't you?"

+ Girls can be more cruel to each other about bisexuality than guys are. In a live version of her song "Drive," Melissa Ferrick says, "If your girlfriend owns more than one towel she's probably straight."

+ When I was online dating and nervous about attending a dance party, a gay girl said to me, "Just wear a dress and be your girly self, and you'll be dancing with a woman in no time." I was stunned. I'd been planning on wearing jeans. I didn't think of myself as "girly." I was vulgar. I bit my nails to the quick. I got acne because of my excess testosterone.

+ This same girl once asked me if I liked hiking. "I love hiking," I said. She made a big show of acting shocked. It was the dumbest thing I'd ever seen. It obviously had everything to do with her, and nothing to do with me.

+ The first person I heard say "I'm not gay or straight, I'm attracted to *people*" was a girl at a new-age camp with a chosen name of Tiger.

+ Being a five-foot-three, average-looking blond chick has its pros and cons. You can become invisible or visible. But the shitty parts are the days you want to be seen and you are not seen, or the days you want to be unseen and you are seen.

+ The morning after having sex with a woman, I got my hair cut. "Sooooooo, do you have a boyfriend?" my hairdresser asked me. "No," I said. "Isn't it so hard to meet men?" he said.

+ When SCOTUS passed same-sex marriage, I was in Austin visiting a friend. She got the alert as we walked into Cafe Magnolia. I wanted to eat there because a scene in the movie *Boyhood* was filmed there. Later at home, her seven-year-old daughter hung out in the kitchen with us. "She wasn't as excited as I was," her dad said. "She just thinks that's how it should be, so it's not a big deal to her." I felt exactly the same. It reminded me of this time in high school when everyone was wearing wristbands about something political. I forget what it was now. Amanda laughed when she saw me wearing one. "It's funny when *you* wear one," she said, "because you don't really care."

+ At a writing retreat in California, I drank countless glasses of wine, putting myself in a vulnerable and dark state of mind. I was sitting around the fire with some writers, talking about

sexuality. "At the end of the day, you *know*," one woman said.
I burst into tears. In front of everyone. Partly drunk, partly
still devastated from my last relationship, partly because
I'd just finished a book (unpublished at this point) about a
not-knowing narrator. I myself did not know. At the end of
the day, I did not know. And it was causing me strife, grief,
extreme distress. I used to know myself so well. Maybe
someday I would, again, but on this night around the fire
in California, I did not.

Maggie and Me: A Love Story

I loved my friend.
He went away from me.
There's nothing more to say.
The poem ends,
Soft as it began—
I loved my friend.

—LANGSTON HUGHES

IN MY BEDROOM THAT I PAINTED blue so I would eat less and write more, a friend sends me a link to the poem "Diary of an Emotional Idiot" by the slam poet Maggie Estep. I've never seen anything like it before and send friends the video of Maggie performing it live. "Is this Alanis Morissette?" my friend Rain asks. "Did you write this?" Simon asks. "Even if you didn't, it's incredible!" I am living in Seattle, and it's 2011.

At yoga one night, I see a flyer with the updated class and schedule times. A woman named Maggie Estep is teaching a sunrise class. Maggie Estep. The same Maggie Estep? Her bio says she lives in Woodstock. I live in Hudson. It's 2012.

I attend the sunrise class. Maggie has a trendy haircut that covers her eyes in a mysterious way. It's a New York City haircut, not an upstate one. Instead of the form-fitting tank tops most wear to yoga, she wears a red T-shirt that reads CBGB. Instead of playing bhajans, she plays "Dancing Barefoot" by Patti Smith. When I am in triangle pose, looking up, as I was taught you are supposed to do, Maggie walks over to me and asks, "Does that feel good on your neck?" No. Not really. "Then don't freaking do it," she says, laughs, and walks away.

After class I introduce myself. I have no memory of this, but two years later when we become friends, she tells me I did. I move to Portland, Oregon, about a week after the class and forget about Maggie, aside from buying *The KGB Bar Reader* anthology because she had a story in it.

While in Portland, I am asked to contribute to an essay collection called *Goodbye to All That: Writers on Loving and Leaving New York*. I notice Maggie is also on the list of contributors. The book will release in October 2013.

A year later, after the book release and having had enough of Portland, I book a red-eye flight back to New York for November 22, 2013. I pack at my friend Eliza's house and give her some of my books to hang on to.

"Hey," Eliza says.

"Yeah?" I look over, and she has her finger on a page of *Goodbye to All That*.

"Do you know this person?" she asks, her voice serious, her finger on Maggie's name in the table of contents.

"Not really but I've met her. She teaches yoga in Hudson. She wears a CBGB shirt. I think she was famous in the eighties."

Eliza disappears upstairs to her attic. She comes back with a cassette tape that reads *No More Mr. Nice Girl: Maggie Estep*. Eliza, who is normally not as obsessive and impassioned as me, obviously feels strongly about this. She explains there was a year in her life she listened to this tape every day. We play the cassette while I finish packing. Eliza sings every word. We look up Maggie's bio on the yoga studio website. Ashtanga yoga on Monday nights.

"I bet her class is really hard," Eliza says.

"You think?" I ask.

"You guys probably have a lot in common," Eliza says.

"You think?" I repeat.

"Yeah. Yoga. Writing. The stuff you both write about."

A few days after I move back to Hudson, an article about the *Goodbye to All That* anthology comes out in the Sunday *New York Times*. It quotes my essay and mentions Maggie Estep. I find Maggie on Twitter and see she's written a blog post about this, a beautiful and honest piece about how there was a time the NYT would do profile pieces on her, and now all she gets is a little mention. The blog post is called "What Kind of Jerk Am I?" "What kind of an attention-craving jerk am I to be offended that there aren't several paragraphs devoted to ME?" she writes.

That Tuesday night, I attend a hot vinyasa class. I think I spy Maggie across the room from me. That red T-shirt again. When class is over she struts toward me.

"Hey. I thought you were in Oregon," she laughs. "I just made it sound like you were in a cult!"

"I moved back. How did you know I was living there?"

"Your essay in *Goodbye to All That*," she answers. "I moved to Hudson right after you moved to Portland, and when I got here, everyone would mention you to me. Because we both write shit. Apparently, we're supposed to be friends."

She puts on her fur coat. She smells of gum and perfume and dog. She puts on lip gloss. (She is never not wearing lip gloss.) We exchange numbers; she tells me she teaches yoga on Monday nights and that I should come. We walk down the street together—we live two blocks apart.

We begin texting every day, going to yoga twice a week, chatting about books we are writing and reading. It's like that in small towns, especially when you're both female writers.

There was a point in the eighties when Maggie was THE female writer. The *New York Times* liked to call her a "spoken-word star." Before feminism was Twitter-trendy, Maggie was putting out work like "Car Guy" and "The Stupid Jerk I'm Obsessed With," breaking doors down for female authors like me. She was personal, political, dirty. She didn't hold back, and she was respected for that. She wrote directly and powerfully about addiction, queers, snorting and shooting drugs, fucking stupid men and dyke-y women in an astute and poignant way. "I'm a Masturbating Idiot and a Sexual Neanderthal. Welcome to my life," she writes in *Diary of an Emotional Idiot*. She gave an important voice to not-normal girls, speaking to them and for them.

"I can't believe MAGGIE ESTEP is your neighbor," a few friends tell me.

Neither can I. I know this is a stroke of insane luck. At fifty, Maggie had published seven novels and two spoken-word CDs. And everything she produces is good. She is a real-deal artist. The year I was born, 1986, she was at the Jack Kerouac School of Disembodied Poetics. She's lived the gritty life in New York City. She's gone to rehab and recovered from using heroin. There is something surreal about meeting a writer whose work I've long respected, something magical about how she exceeds my expectations. She's had a unique and enviable past, and I want to hear everything about it.

I am a regular at Maggie's Monday night class. She plays a mix of Patti Smith, the Magnetic Fields, and Fleet Foxes. She has us chant before class. I can't help thinking about how funny it is to be singing with Maggie Estep and how now she is singing songs about Shiva and Ganesha instead of shouting and slamming "Scab Maids on Speed" or "Sex Goddess of the Western Hemisphere."

Maggie and I skip Hudson's Winter Walk, and instead I go along with her to where she is doing a reading at the Golden Notebook in Woodstock. She offers to drive, so we get into her car with her dog, Mickey, in the back. At the reading, someone asks me if I know Maggie. "Yes, I came with her," I say proudly. I tell Maggie this on the ride home and she says, "Does he not realize we're cohorts?"

Maggie and I meet on the street corner one night and swap books. She says she wants to read my essay collection over Christmas at her mom's. For a while she's been telling me she has no copies of her own books, but she might have them at her exes' houses. Then she thinks maybe she has some copies in French or German. But finally she finds a copy of *Alice Fantastic*. She signs the book with a Sharpie: *Darling Chloe, I always think if Lou Reed was alive he'd write a Darling Chloe song about you.*

During these months we are friends, we are supposed to go for tea, and I am going to interview her. We try to choose a day to do this, but don't commit. On the street corner that night, I tell her, "Well, I'm free all the time."

"I don't do much either. I work at the real estate firm only two days a week," she says. "I also spend the days writing and going to yoga."

Maggie doesn't like her apartment because it has bamboo floors, and I'm living at home at my dad's. She e-mails me: *Do you wanna give being roommates a shot? Two women writing and going to yoga could, after all, be the next sitcom. 21st century Seinfeld style.*

One Monday night at yoga she announces she is in a weird mood because her friend Thom has died. She dedicates the class to Thom and lights a candle on the altar. After class I stay with her while she locks up.

I tell her I'm sorry about her friend Thom. She says she kept thinking she wanted to hang out and see Thom. And she'd kept putting it off. "My first reaction was total disbelief. He couldn't possibly be dead. He wasn't old. He was full of life."

On the way out the door, she tells me she can't get to sleep at night. She can't stop reading. "What's so compelling?" I ask her. What can't she put down?

"Malcolm Gladwell and Will Self."

"Do you ever think about writing a memoir?" I ask.

"Yeah. About men. The men I've dated."

. . .

Maggie works at a real estate firm right in town so she is always hearing about apartments. We look at a couple of them together, but nothing pans out. She is adamant about wanting a YARD and a TUB. She always capitalizes those words. We keep scouring Craigslist.

. . .

One night after yoga, sitting at the check-in desk, a man named David is talking to us. He is teasing Maggie, saying, "Let me guess, you have to go home and WRITE."

Maggie looks at me, rolls her eyes. "People think we just sit around and eat bonbons, which we do sometimes," she says.

David asks me if I am a writer too. "How many books do you have?" I tell him I have one. He begins to make fun of me—"Maggie's got seven!" Maggie jumps to my side, saying, "She's younger than I was when I put out my first book."

"Where's your new book?" she asks me. "This, coming from the person who is taking, so far, five years between books," she says.

On New Year's Day, Maggie teaches a donation-based class, donating the proceeds to pit bull rescues. When I am in full backbend, wearing my green leggings, Maggie walks over to me and says, "Hi, Gumby."

I start dating Daniel, who lives in Brooklyn. Maggie sees me at hot yoga, asks if she can take my photo because I am wearing all green and purple, one of those ridiculous yoga outfits you find yourself in in the middle of winter, when you are rarely changing out of leggings.

"I love your outfit," she says. "My ex-boyfriend slash best friend, John, is coming to town next Saturday, and I want you to come to dinner with us." I remember thinking this was such a quirky and generous invitation. I tell her I'd begun seeing someone, could he come too? Of course.

"Bring Daniel to yoga so we can judge him," she says, and I do.

◆ ◆ ◆

Maggie e-mails: *I won't make yoga today. I woke up at 6 convinced I was dying (had this weird horrible burning in my chest) and actually contemplated going to the hospital, then managed to fall back asleep and slept too late, though at least I am not dead and mysterious chest burning is gone.*

I'm so glad you're not dead! I respond.

A few nights later, we go to dinner at a ramen restaurant with John and Daniel. I sit across from Maggie. We both have tofu and noodles. She orders rice pudding afterwards for everyone to split. I'd been reading her book *Diary of an Emotional Idiot*, and there's a line in it where the narrator says masturbation is a great way to get the motivation to vacuum. I bring this up, for table conversation. *What?* the guys ask.

"Masturbating," Maggie explains. "It makes you want to vacuum." We laugh. The guys say nothing.

I ordered her other books online. I listened to her albums. I can tell I am talking and gushing about her too much to anyone who will listen. I listen to her poem "Car Guy" constantly:

So I'm riding my bike down 50th and this guy rolls down his window and looks up at me and says, "Hey! Bike lady!"

So I look down at him and I go, "Hey! Car guy!"

Maggie plays the song "White Winter Hymnal" by Fleet Foxes in every yoga class, and then I begin hearing it everywhere. In an Irish pub near midtown in the bathroom. At a coffee shop in Bed-Stuy, it comes on again.

How are you? I text Maggie early one morning.

Cold. You?

Cold. Sorry if I woke you.

Never. Hell, I'm up with the sun.

Maggie and I have a reading at Oblong Books in Rhinebeck for the *Goodbye to All That* book. *Wait, is this a panel?* she e-mails me. *I HATE panels.*

While getting ready for the reading, my self-esteem plummets. I text Maggie. *Anxiety about my acne. This too shall pass?*

She replies within a beat, like a true spoken-word artist: *I'm old and fat and stupid.*

On our way to Rhinebeck, we pull into a gas station for chocolate and coffees. I get out of the car, and Maggie tells me to put a fuck-ton of sugars in her coffee. I worry three aren't enough for her, so I put two more packets into my coat pocket, in case.

Maggie takes a sip of her coffee and announces, "This coffee is vile." She says the Rolos are stale but keeps asking for them, holding open her fingerless-gloved hand. I tell her about the dream I'd had the night before, something about having to insert a glitter kit into my vagina.

"I don't know what the eff was up with that dream," I say.

"You know, you can actually say *fuck* in my car," Maggie says.

Later, when I describe someone as a "biatch," she says, "You can say *bitch* in my car too."

You wouldn't know Maggie hates panels when we sit down in front of the audience. She charms everyone's pants off. I am reading next to a *performer*, which is so much different than a writer who can read her work. During the Q&A, we are still drinking our gas-station coffees. We take our gum out of our mouths and place it, classily, on the lids of our cups. I ask Maggie if she wears a helmet when she rides her bike all over New York City, like she describes in her essay. She looks at me and says, deadpan, "No. I was an organ donor." The crowd laughs.

After the reading we mingle for a while. Someone takes our photo, and in it we are clearly laughing loudly, smiling huge, arms tight around each other, both dressed in black. She posts it on her Facebook page, *With Darling Chloe last night at Oblong Books.* I post it on Twitter and call it *Caffeinated Lovebirds.*

It is the last reading Maggie will do, and most likely the last photograph ever taken of her conscious. When she dies, three days later, *USA Today* publishes the photo.

•   •   •

After the reading, she drops me off at home. I tell her I go to bed early these days, super different than how I used to live my life. "Like, you used to do drugs and fuck strangers?" she asks. "Me too. But tonight I'm going to eat a container of Coconut Bliss ice cream and write. Lame." We laugh. I say thanks for the ride, leave the car.

The last place I see her is the first place I saw her. On little sleep, I run up the stairs to the yoga studio. Maggie is sitting at the desk. "Long time no see," I say.

In Warrior 1 pose, Maggie walks over to me and adjusts my body. "Fix me," I joke to her. She looks into my eyes and smiles. It is our last in-person interaction. I don't say good-bye when class is over; I just book it down the stairs.

While waiting for Daniel to arrive that night, I am texting with Maggie.

Am I a stupid yoga jerk? she asks.

What do you mean? I say.

I mean, when I am teaching class, do you think, God what an idiot? I tell her no. I tell her I think she sounds like she knows what she's doing and talking about, and that she's a wonderful yoga teacher.

God, I love you, she responds.

I love you too! I write.

Sunday morning, lying in bed, Daniel and I watch videos of Maggie performing. I've drawn Daniel into my infatuation with Maggie and he's reading her novel *Hex*. "Maybe we should see if she wants to get coffee," I mumble at one point, but don't text her.

Around three p.m. my phone rings: Maggie. I figure she's calling to remind me to go to yoga tonight or wants to grab lunch or has found an apartment for us to look at. I say hello. But it is a male voice on the other line. It is Maggie's ex-boyfriend. "Do you know who I am?" he asks. "Maggie and I were just hanging out at my place and she had a heart attack. I took her to the ER, and now she's being transported by medevac to the Albany Medical Center. Will you drive to the hospital with me?" He picks me up twenty minutes later.

At the hospital, Maggie's best friend—who Maggie calls Laura the Hot Farmer—is already there. The three of us, ex-boyfriend, best friend, and me, the new friend, sit around until midnight. We say we'll start a blog about our hospital visits for her to read when she wakes up. We will document everything. She will laugh when she reads it.

We drive to the hospital again the next day with apples and potato chips. The doctors let us in to see Maggie, who is being cooled down and then heated back up. She's in a coma. Someone takes a photo. We will show her, when she wakes up. How crazy it all is. How many wires and machines she is hooked up to. She looks tiny, pale.

When the doctor visits us in the waiting room, I know from his (her? I've blocked her out of my mind) expression it is serious. She/he is warning us.

But she is the picture of health, we tell the doctors. *But she is a yoga teacher. But sometimes she teaches yoga and goes to the gym in the same day. But she's been sober for twenty years. But she is vegan*, we whine.

Maggie calls the names she has for her friends *monikers*. In the car on the way home from the hospital after midnight, during a bleak silence on the highway, Maggie's ex-boyfriend turns to look at me.

"You should know, Maggie's name for you is *My New* BFF. She is always saying she has to see what the New BFF is up to."

I don't go to the hospital the next day. I have to teach my class for teens, the one Maggie had talked about at dinner. There'd been a blizzard; there are so many blizzards this winter, it is a white winter hymnal, and many of my students do not show. The class releases at four p.m. and I curl up into a fetal position on my couch and fall asleep in all of my clothes. My hat. Aching. Knowing.

At seven in the morning my phone rings. It's Laura the Hot Farmer.

"Maggie died last night." It is February 13, 2014.

Laura invites me over to the ex-boyfriend's apartment. The light outside is too bright, like coming down from an acid trip, or when you finally leave the house after a weeklong flu and everything is too real and cartoonish. I stick my gloveless hands into my coat pockets for warmth. My heart cracks in half when I feel the Domino sugar packets for Maggie from three days ago.

I don't stop shitting all day. There are donuts and fruit on the table we all sit around. People drop by. It's a crystal cold clear freezing day. As I shit in her ex-boyfriend's bathroom, I don't

know what to think. We sit at the table, make lists, plan the
memorial. Someone dies, and suddenly it's "Who's gonna design
the flyer?"

We walk to Maggie's apartment to choose what she'll wear. I
hold the leash of her dog, who bolts up her stairs. We choose silver
hoop earrings and a burgundy shirt. When no one is looking, I
steal a shiny sequined bracelet, shove it in my coat pocket. Her
ex-boyfriend lies on her bed. "Remember dinner a few weeks
ago?" he says.

Just like that she's dead.

I drive to the burial alone, through the flurries, leave Daniel
in bed. The roads are slippery. I borrow a black dress from a
friend. I wear a leather jacket and yellow hat. Crosby, Stills &
Nash plays on the radio. We stand in the snow in the graveyard. I
recognize people from yoga class. I see David, the one who asked
me how many books I have. We hug. I know almost no one there.
I see the owner of the yoga studio where Maggie taught. She says
a few words, about how some people are suns and some people
are moons, but then there was Maggie, who was a shooting star.

"This is a tender time," she says. "The harshness of February
continues, and we are yearning for spring. Crocuses, snowdrops,
lungwort, Christmas rose, the flowers of spring will yet return,
will push up with their indomitable energy to live and in the
meantime . . . we'll weep."

I am weeping with my arms wrapped around my body. I am profoundly grateful when Laura the Hot Farmer comes up behind
me and wraps her arms around me through the rest of the service. She gives me rose petals to put on the casket. She says, "You
look hot. Maggie would be proud." We put sticks of gum and rose
petals into the casket. It's lowered into the ground and we drive
to the memorial.

At the memorial, I am in a foul mood. It's eleven in the morning. My boyfriend keeps touching my leg and shoulder, and all
I can think is Maggie's line: "Don't TOUCH me, what am I your
fucking CAT?" John S. Hall spits poetry. Stephin Merritt plays

"The Book of Love." Steve Buscemi makes a surprise appearance, reads e-mails between Maggie and himself. He admits he didn't respond to her last e-mail. At Maggie's memorial I receive an e-mail that my new book will, in fact, be published. One week later I find an apartment with a YARD and a claw-foot TUB.

"I think you got those good things because of Maggie," my friend Fran says. I dedicate the book to Maggie.

In the first week or two after her death, Daniel and I are never awake more than ten minutes before we watch videos of Maggie. We watch "Happy" and listen to "Car Guy" and "Pee Lady." On his computer, I see an e-mail over his shoulder that reads, *Sorry this is late. My girlfriend's friend died.* Both of the labels make me nauseated. I leave the bed for the bathroom and sit with my head between my hands. Flip through one of the copies of *Men's Health.*

I'm standing on the corner of Lorimer and Metropolitan Avenue, talking on the phone to Fran in a snowstorm. I've left Daniel's bed to buy some ginger ale and oranges because he has the flu from quitting smoking, which, apparently, is a thing. I'm freezing, but I pace around the streets. I'm still pulsating with adrenaline from the memorial and describing it to her.

"Well, what's gonna happen now?" Fran asks.

"What do you mean?"

"I'm worried you're gonna get, like, depressed."

"Probably."

Three weeks after Maggie's death, Laura and I drive to where she is buried, though there is still no tombstone. We stand outside, holding our coffees. "She's not here," Laura says. It begins to drizzle.

Six months later, in August, there is finally a tombstone. I can't find it. I'm driving all over the goddamn graveyard, the sun in my face. I break down and text Maggie's ex. He tells me the number of it, directs me via text to it. Asks me to send him a photo of it. Finally, I arrive. I park the car and get out. *Maggie Estep: Writer and Friend.*

I use up all of the ink in my printer printing a high-resolution photo of Maggie.

Where's your new book, darling Chloe?

I think this is the year we both get big book deals.

I have an idea: let's put books out at the same time and go on a book tour together.

See you tonight at hot and smelly yoga?

I found us an apartment—it might be skanky but I'm o.k. with fairly serious skank. You?

I've lost friends to death before, and it's always terrible, but at least I'd known them. It is different with Maggie; we were just starting our relationship. We had plans to live together, to have tea and do an interview together, to put out books at the same time and go on tour together. As soon as she came into my life, I knew my life had gotten better and would continue to get better as I continued to get closer to her. I'd gotten through my life without knowing Maggie, but when I met Maggie, I felt relief. I could relax. And then, as mysteriously as she swooped in, she inscrutably disappeared.

At a comedy club in Los Angeles, I see Marc Maron perform. I walk to the bathroom and pass him in the hallway. We make eye contact and say hi. Maggie's voice is in my ear saying, "I made out with Marc Maron in the eighties. Comedians are worse than writers."

After significant struggle, I am finally going to yoga again. There is a framed photo of Maggie and her dog, Mickey, on the altar. They are kissing. No matter where I am in the room, I know my proximity to the photo, whether I can only see the corner of the frame or Mickey's white fur. More often than not, I plant my mat in the front row. I hate being there, while knowing that if I want to be near her, I have to be. This is where Maggie is, if she's anywhere. I bite the insides of my cheeks. My fingers dig into the mat. I glance at the photo, feeling both viciously angry and profoundly grateful for the luck I've had. I leave the room and walk through the lobby to the bathroom. During the holidays, there are Hershey's Kisses and clementines in the lobby; Maggie and I ducked out of yoga a few times and ate a few of the chocolates during class. Laughing.

When I walk around Hudson, I am forced to walk by her old apartment. The restaurant we had dinner at. Both yoga studios we frequented. The corner we swapped books on. Some days I do not leave the house until late afternoon after writing. On these days, I haven't used my speaking voice yet or made eye contact with anyone. At night I will go to yoga. It reminds me of Maggie. The special thing about her was that she was the one woman in my life who didn't need a partner, who told me she wanted to live with her pit bull for the rest of her life. She made being a loner legitimate and cool. She was my person. We would have been friends forever, but I am changed from being her friend for the short time that I was. She was my New BFF too.

"I know you might think this is eccentric and woo-woo," Maggie told the yoga class one night. "But singing is good. Like, REALLY good. It's the healthiest thing you can do." Then she lit the candles on the altar, bowed to the ground, walked barefoot— her red toenails freshly painted—to the sound system, pushed play and turned up Patti Smith, and began teaching us.

I understand that Maggie's well-known poem "Happy" is sarcastic satire. But after knowing Maggie, I'm beginning to question that. She walks on stage, radiant, with her unmistakable commanding energy. All she has to say is "This is called 'Happy,'" and her delivery makes the audience chuckle. Maggie throws her head back and laughs with them. That signature laugh, her beautiful mouth wide. It gives me shivers.

The last line of the poem is how I like to remember Maggie:
To hell with sticking my head in the oven, I'm happy
I'm a radiant asshole and I'm happy
I've got joy shooting from the roots of my hair down to my violent red toenails
I'm happy to be here to be alive to be here to be alive
I'm here, I'm alive
and I'm happy

Berlin 2009

I WAS SUPPOSED to stay in Berlin for five nights, but I stayed for three months. My dad had suggested I go to visit my brother, Trevor. Maybe it would be good for me, he said. His attitude is always "just do it," like *Nike*, so we booked a flight.

I was twenty-three and experiencing profound boundary issues and confusion. I'd fallen in lust with a man nine years older than I was, who didn't believe in monogamy and who would not share things with me, things like T-shirts or books or bites of his dinner. I was dying for a man to give me a T-shirt or a book or a bite of his dinner. Simon was giving and generous emotionally and sexually and in every other way. We'd been in this ambiguous and turbulent relationship for two years, after meeting in a nonfiction writing class where he'd written about his cocaine overdose—a causality of his mother's deathly illness—and I'd written about my heroin dabbling and friend who committed suicide by hanging himself. We bonded immediately and intensely, but the circumstances of uncertainty were wearing me down. I hated how he never remembered my birthday.

I'd left New York City a month earlier. I thought if I didn't, I would die. I would wake up thirty-five years old and an alcoholic, or I'd get hit by a taxi, or I'd snort a drug that would kill me on the spot. So I quit my job at the jewelry store, got a big tattoo of red train tracks (including the third rail) on my back, and left the yellow bedroom I rented in Inwood.

A few days before I flew to Berlin, I went to visit Simon in the East Village. While I waited for him to get out of work, I drank a decent amount of whiskey at various bars around Alphabet City, then went to a gallery to see an exhibit on the performance artist

Sophie Calle. I'd read a review in the *New York Times* saying that Calle's art often involves invading the privacy of others, and I loved her immediately. In the guest book I told her this much and wrote my e-mail address. My writing wasn't legible, as I was drunk. I never heard from her, not that I expected to.

Simon. I often couldn't sleep the nights before we were going to see each other, my stomach giving me giddy Christmas-morning butterflies. He was different from most men I'd known; his eyes shone and his body was flexible and he liked processing his emotions and he had a therapist he went to each week in White Plains. I carried a different book at all times to give him. He didn't give me books. "I don't give you books because I don't give anyone books," he said. "I'm too anal for that and you know it. It has nothing to do with your importance to me." Our love was familial. "You're like my sister, but my sister that I want to fuck!" he exclaimed more than once, drunk and high and happy. We sat in dozens of East Village dives talking about how lucky we were to have found each other.

We had one of our usual nights. We went out for ice cream cones and smoked weed after sex. We giggled and sang along to Bonnie Prince Billy. In the morning, we both started getting depressed. He'd just moved into a new apartment and the bedroom was dark with a slant of a window, which you could only see cement out of. We called his room "The Well."

"I think a windowless room affects us more than we think," I said.

"Yeah. Everything affects us more than we think."

When Simon left to shower I reached down in between the bed and the wall, looking for my underwear but pulled up someone else's. They were tiny and light blue, with a small pink bow. From Target. Simon and I never discussed being exclusive, but I was still crushed to my core. He made breakfast and it was too spicy and my nervous system was screwed and I kept having to go to the bathroom. I went to the bodega to buy more toilet paper. It was fucking hot. I kept changing my clothes.

Simon was about to leave to visit his parents upstate. We'd grown up on opposite sides of the Hudson River. He'd recently bought a motorcycle. I stood outside on Ninth Street with him, and he asked me to hold his helmet for a second, and I accidentally dropped it on the hot pavement and it cracked. "Fuck!" he yelled.

That night, I slept at his apartment, and my friend Rain came over because I didn't want to be alone. Rain had recently "gone crazy," as she put it. She'd accidentally smoked PCP and the NYPD found her crawling around in Central Park and put her on a bus to Massachusetts. She woke up in a psych ward in Boston on her twenty-third birthday.

Rain was thinking about going to Berlin too. She'd just gotten out of a relationship and didn't really have anywhere else to go. "Let's go to Berlin!" we said. We went to Lucy's on Avenue A, where we met some guys that told us, "If you like New York, you'll *love* Berlin."

Later that night, Rain and I sat outside smoking and drinking beer on Simon's steps, listening to *Blood on the Tracks* on the small tape player I always carried with me. I told Rain about the underwear and about how Simon wasn't sharing enough with me. Why could I be so intimate with him and not have free reign over his T-shirt drawer? If he could make me orgasm, why couldn't I borrow his books? It might have been stupid logic, but it was my logic nonetheless. I had nothing of his to hold on to. Not a piece of paper or a sweatshirt or a book. What I was really saying was *He doesn't love me enough.*

It was pouring the next morning, and his cat had vomited on the floor. I wanted to leave it, but I cleaned it up because I loved him. Rain and I stole some of Simon's quarters out of a large jar on top of his fridge to get coffees across the street at MUD.

That afternoon, before I left Simon's apartment, I searched his messenger bag and found one of his journals. I read about him sleeping with a woman with a taut stomach and tight ass and I hurled the journal across the room. It wasn't the first time I'd read his journals, but it would be the last. I texted him about what I'd read, and he replied, *I think you should leave my apartment.* I left, but only after stealing a white T-shirt and more money. There were some colored hard-boiled eggs left over from Easter, eggs I thought about smashing all over the furniture.

I took the train that evening to JFK and went to a bar and drank whiskey. I texted Simon something about how I felt existential, about how I loved him and he would never see me again. He didn't respond. These were the last texts I'd send for months, since my phone would not be activated in Europe. I loved the song "50 Ways to Leave Your Lover" and was pretty proud of my interesting way of leaving. I hadn't even left a note, which felt really badass. I was thrilled to be the one who was leaving, instead of the one who was left.

All I had with me was a red-and-black JanSport backpack. In it was a journal, a pair of shorts, a sweatshirt, and a couple shirts. My hair was in braids. Blond hair from a box.

◆ ◆ ◆

When I arrived in Europe, Trevor and two of his friends met me at the airport. They were hitchhiking around, had been for weeks. I'd never hitchhiked before, but I could tell from the way they were acting there was a high that came along with it. We couldn't hitchhike as a group of four, so we split up into groups of two, and I went with my brother. My brother and I wrote the names of the cities we needed to get to in black marker on slabs of cardboard to hold up. He had me keep his guitar in front of me because "people always pick up a girl with a guitar."

Each time we got into a car, I fell asleep in the backseat. This turned into a routine, one Trevor didn't love. I never sat in the front. I always fell asleep against my window, drooling all over myself.

"It's not fair," he told me. "You just check out and I have to do all the legwork and small talk."

"You're right," I said. "I'll be better next time, I promise." But then I'd fall asleep again.

I keep saying I was going to Berlin, but I'm not sure that was the plan at all. I guess the plan was for me to just travel around with my brother. I flew into Frankfurt and then we hitchhiked around Copenhagen and Austria. My brother and his friends shared everything: bread, Brie, melodicas, and guitars. This was a different planet, so communal and artistic compared to the pavement-and-liquor lifestyle I'd been leading in New York. So innocent and hedonistic in a completely different way.

We took rides from all sorts of people: the Dutch pilot for Lufthansa who told us, "I didn't always look like this. I used to have long hair and earrings." The jolly German tan couple who had their own pot of coffee and mugs in their car. The trans woman who had my brother transfer twenty thousand euros over the phone to his friend while she drove. The woman who used pets as therapy and whose car had a wild west theme. The hippie van of five Italians. I sat down next to one, and he said, "Hi, I'm Mathias. You have to help us finish all of our drugs before we get to Switzerland." The German fifty-year-old who told us he was really into the band Grizzly Bear from Brooklyn and had we heard of them? The guy in the Netherlands who told us he loved George Bush. The Swiss guy who played Eddie Vedder's *Into the Wild* soundtrack for two hours. I liked it the first time, and even the second, but on the fourth I swore to myself I would never listen to Eddie Vedder again.

◆ ◆ ◆

I was unhappy. Destabilized. At a Turkish grocery store in Frankfurt, I saw a box of hair dye. The color was called Bordeaux. I wanted to be like Kate Winslet in *Eternal Sunshine of the Spotless Mind*. I bought the box of hair color but couldn't actually go through with it, though I let a German girl give me an unbecoming cut—she cut it to my chin with dull scissors in her bedroom.

The night before I was supposed to fly back to New York, my brother proposed I go back to Berlin with him and stay however long. I decided to stay. My gut said no, but something else said

yes. Plus, Rain was coming. I was excited—take THAT, Simon!
I'm exciting and unpredictable! I share with people! I don't believe
in privacy! I am so adventurous I am moving to Europe!

After more traveling, staying on a houseboat in Amsterdam,
eating space cakes in Amsterdam, we hitchhiked "home" to my
brother's flat in Berlin. Trevor shared a place with a few people
from various parts of the world, and they called it the Big Pink.
And it was big and pink. There was a tiny kitchen in which they
all cooked and baked, and they did it well. I slept on a futon in
the living room. Each morning when I woke, I stared at a clock
on which the hands moved backwards, and a cardboard slab that
read BERLIN in black marker. Rain was to arrive in a week. There
was an air mattress ready for her.

In my e-mails from this time, I see I requested that Rain bring
me not more jeans or underwear or even more books—I asked
her to bring me mascara, cassette tapes, and a hair straightener.
Trevor asked her for brown sugar, which was almost impossible
to find in Berlin, and his favorite kind of pen.

◆ ◆ ◆

I was always e-mailing Rain and asking her to check my messages
on my cell phone since I couldn't from Europe. I was sure Simon
was trying to get in touch with me. "It says no messages, dude,"
she'd tell me every time.

◆ ◆ ◆

When Rain arrived, we decided to hitchhike to Denmark to attend
the Roskilde music festival. My brother figured out we could go for
free if we volunteered. So we were friskers. We had four-hour shifts
each day and had to wear neon-orange vests. People weren't allowed
to bring in food or alcohol, and whatever we found on them, we
could keep. So we were never out of alcohol.

We saw Fleet Foxes cover "Dreams" by Fleetwood Mac. We
saw Kanye West and Nine Inch Nails. We saw Lucinda Williams

and Fever Ray. We saw Nick Cave & the Bad Seeds and we saw Oasis and the Yeah Yeah Yeahs.

Sounds epic on paper but in real life Rain and I both got our periods as soon as we got there. We didn't have any tampons or pads. Dehydrated, bleeding, and stressed, we asked the girls camping near our tent if they could help us. One said she had exactly two tampons but couldn't give them to us *in case* she got her period. We were certain we would lose each other and die in a field somewhere, bleeding and alone.

Rain and I were besotted with the tan and blond Danish girls who didn't have a hair on their bodies. One morning I woke up and the first thing I saw was a perfect tan ass in a thong belonging to a beautiful Danish woman.

This made us feel worse about ourselves. I had that unbecoming haircut and had gained weight from the beer and homemade bagels that were always available at the Big Pink. Life was more sedentary—in New York I walked miles each day; here, I barely walked. And when we hitchhiked, we brought with us a baguette, Brie, and Nutella. I was getting fat.

On the last day of Roskilde we walked around the fairgrounds. It was like the scene in *Charlotte's Web* where the rat walks around and sings, *A fair is a veritable smorgasbord orgasbord orgasbord, after the crowds have ceased. Each night when the lights go out, it can be found on the ground all around. Oh, what a ratly feast!* We found food and euros and a pair of brand-new green Doc Martens that didn't fit any of us, but we were excited by the idea that we could sell them. We lugged them around all summer and never sold them.

After Roskilde, Rain and I lived for a few weeks in my brother's living room and searched for an apartment to sublet. When we left the house, we spent our time at a playground made for adults. We drank bottles of Radlermass and sat on a wooden structure filled with sand. It was shaped like a boat with a table in between, two logs for seats. We listened to cassettes we took from the free shop. We had Radiohead's *Pablo Honey* and Green Day's *Dookie.*

After the huge deal I'd made about sharing and privacy in New York, it turned out I wasn't yet comfortable with communal meals at the Big Pink and this whole "living well" way of life. Rain and I were used to Brooklyn, where we could be loud and aggressive and binge drink. It was difficult for me to be in my brother's shadow. Berlin agreed with him, almost as much as it disagreed with me.

Rain and I spent the long afternoons waiting in parks for the one-euro all-you-can-drink wine bar to open up and feed us; we craved that exact orange-pesto-soaked pasta we found totally unappetizing the week before. One night we ate and drank for hours and got in trouble when we left for not paying enough. My dreams were vivid in Berlin, so I wrote them down in the mornings.

Had a dream the God/President of Europe told Rain if we got in trouble one more time for being loud or getting too drunk, we will be kicked out of Europe.

We loved visiting the free shop, and one day we were offered Turkish tea by the two French dudes, Pete and Bruno, who managed and slept in the store.

"We were living in a squat," explained Bruno, "but a group of Germans in their early twenties took over." So the store was all they had left. They slept on the floor.

"But most things here take care of themselves," he said. "We just sit around and drink tea and smoke."

He asked if we had any weed. We didn't. Pete produced a second cup of tea. Some crusty punks and some dogs came in. Bruno filled a large metal bowl with water for the dogs. The dogs were big, leashless things, but nice.

There was a place called the Project House where thirty or forty people lived. They all slept in one room, cooked, divided up chores, and had a workspace with computers. To live there you had to be extensively interviewed. If you had told me about this place when I lived in New York City, I'd have told you it was my dream house. I would have lived there in a second. But now that I had the opportunity, I felt it would be insanely stressful to live that way. Rain and I went to their events, movies and chocolate night, hair-cutting night, but no one talked to us much, and I always left feeling inadequate. "Can my sister have some stuff out of the free shop," I heard my brother ask. "She came here with nothing."

Everything I wanted and tons of opportunities were in front of my face, but I didn't understand how to take them. On Gchat I told my dad I was having a hard time, and he said, *Anywhere is a prison if you let it be.*

◆ ◆ ◆

The sublet Rain and I eventually landed was enormous. The natural light was the best and worst thing about it. The bathroom and bedroom were nothing like the bathrooms and bedrooms we were accustomed to in New York. You could do cartwheels in them. In the bedroom we shared there was one small mattress. Instead of getting another mattress, or futon, or a bigger mattress, we switched off, and whoever wasn't sleeping on it slept on the hardwood floor with a white sheet. There were three cats roaming around, and they liked to jump out the windows, so we always had to remember to close every door behind us and we always forgot. That summer in Berlin was all the days off we'd wished we'd had in New York City. Now we had them, and we had nothing to do. Nowhere to be. Nowhere to go. No cell phones. Eventually I asked my dad to send me his old computer. The computer was broken—it didn't connect to the internet. So I just typed notes on it. When I needed e-mail, I borrowed Rain's computer.

We befriended a German man in his thirties who lived downstairs from us, Christian. He'd recently tried to commit suicide. He liked punk music and introduced me to the Nobunny's music, which I loved. We hung out with him most days, lay on couches watching *Wristcutters*, *Sid and Nancy*, and *Suburbia*. He became a true friend and a dark one. He worked for a porn site, xx.com or something. Sometimes I took his antidepressants for fun, something called Mirtazapine. He warned me it would make me more tired than usual (I was already lethargic from the heat and depression) and give me crazy dreams, but I took it anyway and slept for almost two days. We started spending time with Christian almost every day. We got a kick out of him because he used the phrase "I can't be bothered" often. Rain and I loved the concept and self-indulgence of "I can't be bothered." Finally, there was a phrase for how we'd been spending our days.

Hey girls, what's happening?
Hope you guys had a good time on a Thursday in Berlin!
Please excuse me, but tonight I had to meet those friends of mine on my own . . .
What happened was that I showed up being the only lonely sorry ass motherfucker that kept hiding his sorry ass face behind glasses of vodka/whiskey/schnapps/whatever without actually being in touch with anybody else . . .
I so wished you'd be around!
In the end I destroyed several pieces of furniture, made that one girl cry, made enemies with my friends' boy-/girlfriends, left the place, got picked up by the cops, finally got out of the police station, back home, writing this e-mail . . .
So fucked up that I couldn't possibly be bothered going to work tomorrow, hehehehehehe ;)
Cheers Chloe and Rain, luv ya!

yo how's it going?
just had a chat with patrick and he says he is still unsure about trippin today, but he's got all the shiat and i'm going over to his place around 8 or something . . .
you wanna join? maybe trip, maybe do speed or whatever?

wadddap doooooooodz?!?!?!!!!!???11?

you were right, chloé, i had a good time at the doctor's, she is really keen on chemicals and putting them together like lego blocks, so

I got additional pills, some prozac type high end feel good shit -
sweeeeeeeeeeeet :)
so are you up to anything? please come over if you feel like it!
cya!

◆ ◆ ◆

Rain and I took German acid and German speed. We sat in
drum circles in parks, making temporary friends with strangers.
Sometimes the only activity we did all day was swing on a swing
set, complaining of our uncomfortable underwear. We'd purchased
underwear at a department store, and when we brought it back to
our flat, found out it was children's underwear. They were tiny and
pale blue, and we chose to wear them all summer instead of returning to the store for adult underwear. We couldn't be bothered.

I have a vague memory of going to a protest. We rarely did
anything, so when we did, it felt like an epiphany. I e-mailed the
article about the protest the next morning to both my parents,
telling them I attended it. *Was it a general economic protest?* my
dad wrote back. I didn't answer the e-mail. I didn't have a clue
what the protest was for.

Christian brought us to a library event space called Another
Country, run by a woman named Sophia Raphaeline. She looked
similar to Fred Armisen's character in *Portlandia*, the owner of
the feminist bookstore. You had to pay five euros to be a member of Another Country, and then you could come for the free
dinners served in the basement, where the walls were lined with
science-fiction paperbacks. We ate lasagna and omelets and
chicken and stuffed peppers. You could rent out books and either
return them or not. Rain got *Queer* by William Burroughs, and
I got something I didn't end up reading, I think it was *Lady
Chatterley's Lover*. After dinner, they showed *The No. 1 Ladies'
Detective Agency* and we sat on a couch drinking wine and eating
éclairs while we watched. Numb.

◆ ◆ ◆

Rain and I often had twenty-minute conversations about whether it was three p.m. or seven p.m., and whether it was Thursday or Friday.

I had many bad tattoo ideas. The one I was most married to was a Joan Didion quote. I wanted to ink her words from *The Year of Magical Thinking, Leis go brown, tectonic plates shift, deep currents move, islands vanish, rooms get forgotten*, under my right breast. I knew I was maybe too young to feel so strongly about those words, but I loved the sentiment. At that point, I hadn't forgotten any rooms, I remembered them in vivid detail, and it fascinated me to think that one day I would. Rain and I often talked of getting braided friendship bracelet tattoos around our wrists, another plan we abandoned. We were good at abandoning plans. So far I'd abandoned my flight home, dying my hair Bordeaux, becoming vegetarian, and getting more tattoos. Rain and I couldn't even buy ourselves the right size underwear; God knows what kind of tattoo we could have ended up with.

◆   ◆   ◆

My brother and I pretty much stopped hanging out. He was perhaps slighted I chose Rain over him, and I was slighted because I always felt condescended to in front of his genius radical friends. I remember he once explained to Rain and I the "right" way to do the dishes and use less water.

"He's right, I guess," Rain said later, surprising me, then following it with, "But it's like . . . who fucking cares how to do the dishes correctly?"

◆   ◆   ◆

In New York City, I knew what was up. I thought I was hot shit. I had tons of friends and a cool job. I knew how to pay my National Grid bill and do my online banking. I knew where drinks were two for one. I had sex. Dozens of people would meet me in bars. In Berlin I had no sex drive, I didn't know where a

bookstore was, or the right word for anything, and I didn't have
a way to Google it. I could have asked someone. But I did not. I
was sleeping all the time—we were sleeping all the time. When
I wasn't sleeping on my stomach, I was pretending to be sleeping
on my stomach. Sleeping on your stomach, I've since learned, is the
most harmful position for your body to sleep in.

It wasn't my first trip to Europe. I'd taken other trips there,
and they left dark memories. *Maybe I just get depressed in Europe,*
I thought. It's my major character flaw.

◆ ◆ ◆

We had leisurely mornings, waking up anywhere between eleven
a.m. and five p.m. There was a radio in the kitchen we played
all the time. The station we liked literally called itself "the black
radio station," and it played American rap songs we knew. One
morning one of us dropped the lid to a teapot and it broke. We
assumed it was not a big deal and left a note for our German
roommate, Flora. But she was upset and gave us directions to a
specialist a three-hour train ride away to get it repaired. This was
one of the only days in Berlin we had something to do, a mission.

◆ ◆ ◆

I finally received a letter from Simon. I'd been sending him,
maybe once a month, incoherent, anxiety-ridden, stream-of-
consciousness brain dumps, and sometimes he responded and
sometimes he did not.

He e-mailed me scanned photos of a long letter he typed on his
typewriter. I asked Christian from downstairs to print it out for
me. I read it out loud to Rain and Christian. I kept it in my pocket,
in my bed. *I'm sorry you found those underwear—not because you
found them but because of how they made you feel,* he wrote. *I love
women: fat skinny tall short boring and exciting,* he wrote. *I wish I
was with you on your adventures. I guess I'll have to have my own. But
as usual yours seem better. Why does time equal pain? I remember*

how happy you were back when we met, he wrote. *I'm sorry for every prick of pain I've ever brought to your skin and insides. Sleep well wherever you may be and know that I may not be able to keep you in the way you want me to but that I do love you. Chloe ultimately does what Chloe wants and feels. But she's got to let me do the same.*

◆ ◆ ◆

Rain, Christian, and I took the train to the Baltic Sea. We drank whiskey on the train and the entire time we were there. We buried each other in the sand and passed out overnight on the beach. I collected some stones and shells to give my brother for his birthday. When we got back to Berlin twenty-four hours later, Rain fell asleep and then vomited into an orange bucket by the bed for three days—either sun poisoning or alcohol poisoning. I felt guilty for feeling relived she was sick and sleeping; it was a much needed break from one another. Our bedroom reeked of puke, so I spent my time downstairs watching films with Christian. When Rain felt better, we took silver duct tape and crafted CAN'T BE BOTHERED on our black tank tops, getting a real kick out of ourselves.

I was restless out of my mind and needed money and structure, so I took a job off Craigslist cleaning a woman's apartment. She kept large Buddha statues around and talked on her headset while I worked, until one morning, coming down off of a bad acid trip, I e-mailed her that I couldn't make it in.

◆ ◆ ◆

In the movie *Half Baked*, there's a part where the guy selling weed describes all of his different clients: the hippie girl, and so on. Jon Stewart plays one of the clients and they call him the "everything's better on weed guy." Because he'll be like:
"Have you ever looked at the stars, man?"
"Yeah . . ."

"Have you ever looked at the stars *on weed?*"

Rain and I made up our own version of this, lying in bed one night. When friends in New York Gchatted us, asking how Berlin was, expecting enthused responses and epic stories, we joked that we wanted to respond:

"Have you ever been anxious and depressed?"

"Yeah."

"Have you ever been anxious and depressed *in Berlin?*"

. . .

Earlier in the summer, my brother and I, in optimistic moods, had booked me an August 31 flight from Paris to New York. A week later I converted it to a round trip; it was cheaper that way, and I thought possibly I'd want to visit my family and friends in New York, grab more of my belongings and then head back to Europe. Rain wasn't leaving Berlin for another month, so when our sublet ran out, we found another place. We had a German roommate who'd just visited Canada and said "Canada's awesome!" literally thirty-seven times each day. He smoked cigars inside and loved Coca-Cola and Abercrombie—"Abercrombie's awesome!"—and worked at a bank. August 31 was approaching, so I packed my JanSport backpack and left Rain with Lorenz. I do not remember my bedroom in this sublet, at *all*. So I guess rooms do get forgotten.

My brother and I had to hitchhike to Paris. We weren't in optimistic moods anymore. We got our regular Brie and baguette (I would grow to resent these foods, even now I dislike Brie) and green apples. We stopped to purchase Nutella along the way. "Eat this," my brother shoved it at me. "The chocolate part makes you happy, and the peanut butter part makes you full."

We hitchhiked through Nice, and actually it was lovely, though as usual, I woke up with my period on the day we left. Our grandmother was born and raised in France, and her brother, whom we'd met briefly as kids, lived in an apartment in Nice.

The plan was for him to meet us and take me to the airport. We coordinated via e-mail that he would pick us up at a church.

Patrick took us to his apartment where he made steaks and proudly showed us his whiskey collection. Trevor and I shared a pull-out couch where we had a nice conversation before we fell asleep.

The following day Patrick took us out to lunch. I had barely any money left, so I ordered a pâte à crêpes, while my brother ordered a croque monsieur. I did not realize Patrick was treating us, and silently cursed my brother and his flavorful sandwich and knowledge that Patrick would pay. In the car on the way to the airport, Patrick played Willie Nelson. *On the road again, just can't wait to get on the road again.* He dropped Trevor off on the side of the road to hitchhike back to Berlin.

When I arrived at JFK, it was past eleven p.m. and no trains were running upstate. My cell phone wasn't activated yet. I called Simon from a pay phone because he was the only person I knew in New York who would possibly give me a place to sleep. He didn't answer. He was probably with his girlfriend with the tiny blue Target underwear or asleep.

My backpack and I spent midnight to seven a.m. in Penn Station, which is something I wish upon none of you. I got in trouble multiple times for lying on the floor; the cops told me it wasn't allowed. I probably also got an STD from lying on the floor. I befriended a woman who was also stuck at Penn Station and she took a photograph of me with my disposable camera. I still have it somewhere. I'm wearing camouflage shorts and black-and-gold Nike sneakers. I am lying on the floor with my legs over my backpack. My arm is over my face. My sneakers smelled. But I was almost home. I was getting closer to knowing what that meant.

Reading Guide:
Discussion Questions and
an Interview with Chloe Caldwell

DISCUSSION QUESTIONS

+ You could call *I'll Tell You in Person* a coming-of-adulthood book—parents split up, friendships and jobs come and go, addictions morph from Tic-Tacs to heroin and back again. It's also a book of essays, not a memoir. How does that choice change your experience of the book? What do essays offer that memoir doesn't, and vice versa?

+ How important is it to see the narrator change over the course of the book? Chloe's candor and willingness to admit to missteps is a big part of what people love about her writing—what does it mean for her to evolve as a character without ever perfecting herself?

+ Friendships are perhaps the most passionate relationships in the book—what does it mean for a young woman to focus her attachments on her friends, not potential romantic partners? How does *I'll Tell You in Person* relate to other stories of young women in that way?

+ Movies, music, magazines, and books—culture (pop and otherwise) is the backdrop for so many of the essays in *I'll Tell You in Person*. How did having *The Fresh Prince of Bel-Air* overlap with a story of the author's uncle, or the Magnetic Fields providing a backdrop for her friendship with another writer, add texture to the essays? Did they create a connection for you? Did they tell you something you wouldn't have known otherwise?

AN INTERVIEW WITH CHLOE CALDWELL

Choosing the order of essays in a collection like this seems difficult! How did you choose what order to put them in? Did you move them around a lot?

Breaking the book up into three sections was an idea from the very beginning, but the themes and order of those sections went through a good amount of strife, until finally the order felt "right" to my editors and me. Chronological order would have been the easiest, but it didn't feel right, so we had room to play with it. I would send the manuscript to my editors having changed the arrangement, and then the editors would change it and send it back to me, and so on, until the order fell into place and we stopped touching it. I thought simultaneously about juxtaposition and underlying themes for the grouping. For example, the first essay was the *last* essay, and something about that wasn't working out, so I revamped it, and just thinking of it as an introduction of sorts guided me while I reworked it. The sections also went through many title ideas, but in the end I didn't want to label them. Sequence is so important—just think about mix CDs.

A lot of the essays touch on the theme of what being a writer, especially one who often publishes close-to-the-bone first-person work, does to your life. How are you feeling about that stuff as this book nears publication?

Depends on the day. Ask me at night after I've smoked a little pot and I'll be so paranoid I'll decide to move to Alaska, dye my hair, and never publish again. Ask me over morning coffee and I'll be hypomanic with how much I love my unconventional lifestyle. At the end of the day, though, regardless of the substances I ingest, I am unspeakably grateful that I have the privilege of doing what I love. If I weren't writing, I'd be a very unhappy person. If I weren't publishing, I wouldn't have a chance to connect with people—readers and writers especially—on a deep level. And I wouldn't get to travel nearly as much! Writing and publishing give my life meaning and direction. Keeps me off the streets.

Which of these essays is your favorite, and why?

"Hungry Ghost" was the most fun to write. I laughed a bunch while writing it, which is always a good sign, and the first few drafts flowed out naturally, without force. I never dreaded editing it like I did with some of the other essays. I enjoyed writing "Failing Singing" because quitting and giving up a talent was a subject I'd always wanted to explore, and also the first essay, "In Real Life," because forewords allow you to basically put a huge disclaimer in your book, like, "I know I'm fucked up! I never said I wasn't! My book is imperfect!" I also have a soft spot for "Soul Killer" because it shines a light on gray-area addiction, something I think is important to talk about. My friend calls that essay the gift that keeps on giving, because after putting something like that into the world, there is nowhere to hide.

Which one was the hardest to write, and why?

"The Music and the Boys." I hadn't thought about that phase of my life for at least fifteen years. I was forced to do substantial investigation—emotional accuracy was profoundly important to me. I had both my mom and the main character read early versions and they both helped me fact-check and reminded me of incidents I'd forgotten. When I drafted that essay at a residency, I threw my back out and had to go get a massage. What's that New Agey quote, the body remembers what the mind forgets? The essay about Berlin felt bleak to write at times. It gets to be a bummer sitting at your desk for hours a day, especially in winter, writing and reliving anxiety and depression, trying to make it entertaining.

How did you come up with the title for the book?

I was texting the phrase to people constantly. Because I've lived in various cities, my close girlfriends are scattered all over, and I was getting frustrated with talking on the phone and texting and liked to save up whatever anecdotes I wanted to share with them for the next time I saw them in real life. A couple friends told me it was getting annoying—"You're too into this 'in person' thing!"—so I eventually tried it out for my manuscript. I've always enjoyed essay collection titles like Sloane Crosley's *How Did You Get This Number* and Jonathan Ames's *What's Not to Love?* because they get to have quirky and conversational titles; they don't have to be super serious. It's funny because my other books went through many title ideas and changes, but with *I'll Tell You in Person*, no editors or friends or agents suggested a change or mentioned it at all. It stuck.

What books did you read while you were putting together this collection? Anything that especially spoke to you or influenced your process?

Violation by Sallie Tisdale, *Tiny Ladies in Shiny Pants* by Jill Soloway, *The Boys of My Youth* by Jo Ann Beard, *I'm Special: And Other Lies We Tell Ourselves* by Ryan O'Connell, *How to Grow Up* by Michelle Tea, *What's Not to Love?* and *The Double Life Is Twice as Good* by Jonathan Ames, *The Unspeakable: And Other Subjects of Discussion* and *My Misspent Youth* by Meghan Daum, *Traveling Mercies: Some Thoughts on Faith* by Anne Lamott, *Let's Explore Diabetes with Owls* by David Sedaris, *Chelsea Girls* by Eileen Myles, and *When the Sick Rule the World* by Dodie Bellamy.

Reading essay collections while writing one is truly the best way to cope with feeling like a freak. You're like, "At least I didn't shit my pants in the South of France!" In my mind, I throw these essay writers under the bus with me, and keeping their books in bed with me helps me sleep at night, the way stuffed animals used to.

LITERATURE
is not the same thing as
PUBLISHING

Coffee House Press began as a small letterpress operation in 1972 and has grown into an internationally renowned nonprofit publisher of literary fiction, essay, poetry, and other work that doesn't fit neatly into genre categories.

Coffee House is both a publisher and an arts organization. Through our *Books in Action* program and publications, we've become interdisciplinary collaborators and incubators for new work and audience experiences. Our vision for the future is one where a publisher is a catalyst and connector.

Emily Books is a publishing project and e-book subscription service that champions transgressive, genre-blurring writing by (mostly) women. Its founders are Ruth Curry and Emily Gould.

Funder Acknowledgments

Coffee House Press is an internationally renowned independent book publisher and arts nonprofit based in Minneapolis, MN; through its literary publications and *Books in Action* program, Coffee House acts as a catalyst and connector—between authors and readers, ideas and resources, creativity and community, inspiration and action.

Coffee House Press books are made possible through the generous support of grants and donations from corporate giving programs, state and federal support, family foundations, and the many individuals who believe in the transformational power of literature. This activity is made possible by the voters of Minnesota through a Minnesota State Arts Board Operating Support grant, thanks to the legislative appropriation from the arts and cultural heritage fund and a grant from the Wells Fargo Foundation Minnesota. Coffee House also receives major operating support from the Amazon Literary Partnership, the Bush Foundation, the Jerome Foundation, the McKnight Foundation, Target, and the National Endowment for the Arts (NEA). To find out more about how NEA grants impact individuals and communities, visit www.arts.gov.

Coffee House Press receives additional support from the Alexander Family Foundation; the Archer Bondarenko Munificence Fund; the Elmer L. & Eleanor J. Andersen Foundation; the David & Mary Anderson Family Foundation; the Buuck Family Foundation; the Carolyn Foundation; the Dorsey & Whitney Foundation; Dorsey & Whitney LLP; the Knight Foundation; the Rehael Fund of the Minneapolis Foundation; the Matching Grant Program Fund of the Minneapolis Foundation; the Schwab Charitable Fund; Schwegman, Lundberg & Woessner, P.A.; the Scott Family Foundation; the US Bank Foundation; VSA Minnesota for the Metropolitan Regional Arts Council; the Archie D. & Bertha H. Walker Foundation; and the Woessner Freeman Family Foundation in honor of Allan Kornblum.

The Publisher's Circle of Coffee House Press

Publisher's Circle members make significant contributions to Coffee House Press's annual giving campaign. Understanding that a strong financial base is necessary for the press to meet the challenges and opportunities that arise each year, this group plays a crucial part in the success of Coffee House's mission.

Recent Publisher's Circle members include many anonymous donors, Mr. & Mrs. Rand L. Alexander, Suzanne Allen, Patricia A. Beithon, Bill Berkson & Connie Lewallen, the E. Thomas Binger & Rebecca Rand Fund of the Minneapolis Foundation, Robert & Gail Buuck, Claire Casey, Louise Copeland, Jane Dalrymple-Hollo, Jennifer Kwon Dobbs & Stefan Liess, Mary Ebert & Paul Stembler, Chris Fischbach & Katie Dublinski, Kaywin Feldman & Jim Lutz, Sally French, Jocelyn Hale & Glenn Miller, the Rehael Fund-Roger Hale/Nor Hall of the Minneapolis Foundation, Randy Hartten & Ron Lotz, Jeffrey Hom, Carl & Heidi Horsch, Amy L. Hubbard & Geoffrey J. Kehoe Fund, Kenneth Kahn & Susan Dicker, Stephen & Isabel Keating, Kenneth Koch Literary Estate, Jennifer Komar & Enrique Olivarez, Allan & Cinda Kornblum, Leslie Larson Maheras, Lenfestey Family Foundation, Sarah Lutman & Rob Rudolph, the Carol & Aaron Mack Charitable Fund of the Minneapolis Foundation, George & Olga Mack, Joshua Mack, Gillian McCain, Mary & Malcolm McDermid, Sjur Midness & Briar Andresen, Maureen Millea Smith & Daniel Smith, Peter Nelson & Jennifer Swenson, Marc Porter & James Hennessy, Jeffrey Scherer, Jeffrey Sugerman & Sarah Schultz, Nan G. & Stephen C. Swid, Patricia Tilton, Stu Wilson & Melissa Barker, Warren D. Woessner & Iris C. Freeman, Margaret Wurtele, Joanne Von Blon, and Wayne P. Zink.

For more information about the Publisher's Circle and other ways to support Coffee House Press books, authors, and activities, please visit www.coffeehousepress.org/support or contact us at info@coffeehouse press.org.

I'll Tell You in Person was designed by
Bookmobile Design & Digital Publisher Services.
Text is set in Adobe Jenson Pro, a typeface drawn by
Robert Slimbach and based on late-fifteenth-century
types by the printer Nicolas Jenson.